I0418107

EXECUTIVE FUNCTIONING SKILLS FOR TEENS

A Parent's Guide To Empower Teens To Improve Focus, Get Organized, Set Priorities, and Gain Fundamental Life Skills

---

AMBER PRESTON

.

Contents

Introduction

It's a typical weeknight in the Johnson household. Fourteen-year-old Ethan is sprawled on the couch, his math textbook lying forgotten on the coffee table as he scrolls through his phone. His mother, Megan, stands in the doorway, a mixture of frustration and concern etched on her face.

"Ethan, have you started your homework yet?" she asks, already knowing the answer.

Ethan barely looks up. "I'll do it later, Mom. I've got time."

Megan sighs, remembering the unfinished project that's due tomorrow—the one Ethan swore he'd start days ago. She thinks about his backpack, a jumbled mess of crumpled papers and half-eaten snacks. And she can't help but worry about his grades, which have been slipping despite his obvious intelligence.

If this scene feels all too familiar, you're not alone. Countless parents find themselves in Megan's shoes, watching helplessly as their bright, capable teens struggle to manage their time, stay organized, and reach their full potential. It's a frustrating, often heartbreaking experience that leaves many parents wondering: Why can't my teen just get it together?

The answer lies in a set of crucial cognitive skills known as executive functions. These are the mental processes that enable us to plan, focus attention, remember instructions, and juggle multiple tasks successfully. They're the backbone of effective learning and productivity—and for many teens, they don't come naturally.

That's where this book comes in. It is your roadmap to understanding and nurturing these vital abilities in your teen. Whether your child is struggling with focus and organization or you simply want to give them a head start in life, this book offers the insights and strategies you need to make a real difference.

Why focus on executive functioning skills? Because they're the key to unlocking your teen's potential, both in school and in life. Cortés Pascual et al. (2019), research shows that strong executive functions correlate with:

- Better academic performance
- Higher self-control
- Improved mental health
- Greater success in future careers

In today's fast-paced, distraction-filled world, these skills are more crucial than ever. Teens face a constant barrage of notifications, social media updates, and information overload. Without strong executive functions, it's all too easy to get lost in the noise and lose sight of what's truly important.

But here's the good news: Executive functioning skills can be developed and strengthened with the right support and strategies. And as a parent, you're in the perfect position to provide that support.

This book is designed to empower you with the knowledge and tools you need to guide your teen towards greater focus, organization, and self-management. Here's what you can expect:

- Clear, jargon-free explanations of what executive functioning skills are and why they matter
- Practical, easy-to-implement strategies for boosting these skills in your teen
- Real-world case studies that bring the concepts to life
- Actionable exercises you can do with your teen to practice and reinforce new skills
- Tips for creating a home environment that supports executive function development
- Insights into how these skills impact academic performance, social relationships, and future success
- Guidance on when and how to seek professional help if needed

Each chapter focuses on a specific aspect of executive functioning, from time management and organization to emotional regulation and goal-setting. You'll find a mix of scientific insights, practical advice, and relatable anecdotes that make the information easy to understand and apply.

The strategies in this book are designed to be flexible and adaptable. Every teen is unique, and what works for one may not work for another. That's why there are a variety of approaches, allowing you to find the ones that resonate best with your child's personality and needs.

As you read, you'll notice that my goal is to be supportive, encouraging, and solution-oriented. I understand the challenges you're facing, and I'm here to offer hope and practical help—not judgment or unrealistic promises. I believe in progress over perfection, and I'll show you how to celebrate small wins along the way.

One of the most exciting aspects of working on executive functioning skills is that you can start seeing positive changes quickly. Many parents report noticeable improvements in their teen's behavior and performance within weeks of implementing these strategies. Of course, lasting change takes time and consistent effort, but those initial wins can be incredibly motivating for both you and your teen.

Before we start, a word of encouragement: By picking up this book, you've already taken a crucial step towards supporting your teen's success. Your commitment to understanding and nurturing their executive functioning skills will make a profound difference in their life—not just now, but for years to come.

So, are you ready to begin? To watch your teen grow in confidence, capability, and independence? To reduce family stress and create a more harmonious home environment? To set your child up for success in high school, college, and beyond?

Then let's get started. Turn the page, and take the first step towards empowering your teen with the executive functioning skills they need to thrive. Together, we'll transform those frustrating evenings into opportunities for growth, connection, and achievement.

ONE

Understanding Executive Functioning Skills

Your teen is sitting at the kitchen table, surrounded by open textbooks and half-finished assignments. They've been there for hours, but progress seems nonexistent. Sound familiar? What you're witnessing isn't laziness or a lack of intelligence—it's a struggle with executive functioning skills.

Executive functioning skills are the brain's air traffic control system. Just as air traffic controllers manage the flow of planes on runways and in the sky, these skills help us manage our thoughts, actions, and emotions. They're the mental processes that allow us to plan, focus attention, remember instructions, and juggle multiple tasks efficiently.

But what exactly are these skills? Let's break it down:

1. **Working memory:** This is the ability to hold and manipulate information in our minds. It's like a mental sticky note that helps us remember and work with information in the short term. For teens, this might mean keeping track of multiple steps in a math problem or remembering the key points they want to make in an essay.

2. **Flexible thinking:** This skill allows us to adapt to new situations and think about problems in different ways. It's about being able to shift gears when needed and consider alternative solutions. For example, a teen with good flexible thinking might easily pivot to a new study strategy if their usual method isn't working.

3. **Self-control:** Also known as inhibition, this is the ability to resist impulses and stay focused on tasks. It's what helps teens resist the urge to check their phone every five minutes while doing homework or avoid blurting out answers in class before being called on.

4. **Task initiation:** This is the skill of starting tasks promptly without undue procrastination. It's what gets a teen to open their textbook and start studying, even when they'd rather be doing something else.

5. **Organization and planning:** These skills involve structuring and managing tasks, information, or materials efficiently. This might look like a teen keeping their backpack organized, managing a calendar of assignments and activities, or breaking down a big project into manageable steps.

6. **Time management:** This is the skill of allocating and using time effectively to complete tasks. It's what helps a teen estimate how long an assignment will take, budget their time accordingly, and meet deadlines consistently.

7. **Emotional regulation:** This involves managing emotions to respond appropriately in different situations. It's the ability to stay calm under pressure, handle frustration without outbursts, and maintain a positive attitude in the face of challenges.

8. **Goal setting and prioritization:** These skills involve determining objectives and ranking tasks based on importance and urgency. It's what allows a teen to decide what homework to tackle first or how to balance studying with extracurricular activities.

These skills are distinct from general cognitive or academic abilities. While cognitive skills involve basic mental processes like memory and reasoning, executive functioning skills are about managing and coordinating these processes to achieve goals. It's the difference between knowing what steps to take and actually organizing those steps in a logical order and managing the time required for each.

Think of it this way: cognitive skills are like the individual musicians in an orchestra, each playing their instrument. Executive functioning skills are the conductor, coordinating all these individual elements to create a harmonious performance.

The development of executive functioning skills is a journey that starts in early childhood and continues well into adulthood. In the early years, children begin to develop basic self-control and simple planning abilities. As they enter middle childhood, more complex planning and organizational skills start to emerge. But it's during the teenage years that these skills really come into their own.

Adolescence is a critical period for the development of executive functioning. The teenage brain is undergoing significant changes, particularly in the prefrontal cortex—the area responsible for many executive functions. This period of neural plasticity presents both challenges and opportunities. On one hand, teens may struggle with impulse control and decision-making as their brains develop. On the other hand, this is a prime time for learning and strengthening these crucial skills.

Understanding this developmental trajectory is crucial for parents. It helps us set realistic expectations and provide appropriate support. We can't expect a 13-year-old to have the same level of organizational skills as an adult, but we can nurture the development of these skills in age-appropriate ways.

It's also important to recognize that executive functioning skills don't develop in isolation. They're heavily influenced by a child's environment and experiences. A supportive home environment, with consistent routines and opportunities for practice, can significantly enhance the development of these skills. Conversely, chaos, inconsistency, or lack of support can hinder their growth.

As parents, we play a crucial role in this process. By understanding these skills and actively supporting their development, we can help our teens build a strong foundation for success. In the chapters that follow, we'll explore specific strategies for nurturing each of these skills. But first, let's dive deeper into why these skills matter so much for our teens.

The Role of Executive Functioning in Teen Development

Now, let's consider how these skills impact your teen's daily life. Remember that homework struggle we mentioned earlier? Executive functioning skills are at the heart of it. When it comes to academics, these skills affect:

- Homework completion: Managing time, breaking down assignments, resisting procrastination. A teen with strong executive functioning skills can sit down after school, prioritize their assignments, break them into manageable chunks, and work through them efficiently without getting distracted.
- Studying for exams: Organizing materials, planning study sessions, maintaining focus. This might look like creating a study schedule, gathering all necessary materials, using effective study techniques, and staying focused during review sessions.
- Class participation: Remembering instructions, staying engaged, thinking flexibly. In class, these skills help teens follow along with lessons, contribute to discussions, and adapt to different teaching styles.

But it's not just about school. These skills are crucial for managing daily life and responsibilities. Think about your teen's packed schedule—school, extracurriculars, social commitments, chores. Strong executive functioning skills allow them to juggle these demands without feeling overwhelmed.

For instance, a teen with good time management and organization skills can balance soccer practice, a part-time job, and schoolwork without dropping the ball. They can plan their week, allocate time for each activity, and adjust their schedule as needed. They're less likely to forget about a shift at work or miss a homework deadline because they've developed systems to keep track of their responsibilities.

The benefits extend to social and emotional well-being too. Teens with strong executive functioning skills are better equipped to:

- Build and maintain relationships: They can remember plans with friends, show up on time, and manage conflicts more effectively.
- Handle social interactions: They're better able to read social cues, control impulses in social situations, and adapt their behavior to different social contexts.
- Manage stress: They can break down overwhelming tasks, prioritize self-care, and use strategies to calm themselves when feeling anxious.
- Navigate conflicts: They can think through problems logically, consider different perspectives, and come up with constructive solutions.

These skills contribute to greater emotional resilience. When faced with challenges, teens with strong executive functioning are more likely to approach problems calmly and systematically, rather than becoming overwhelmed or giving up.

On the flip side, weak executive functioning skills can have long-term consequences. They can impact:

- Career success: In the workplace, executive functioning skills are critical. Employees need to manage their time, meet deadlines, adapt to new challenges, and work effectively with others. Teens who struggle with these skills may find it harder to succeed in their chosen careers, potentially leading to job instability and dissatisfaction.
- Independence in adulthood: Many aspects of adult life rely heavily on executive functioning. Managing finances, maintaining a household, and navigating complex social landscapes all require these skills. Teens who haven't developed strong executive functioning may struggle to live independently, relying more on others for support.
- Overall well-being: Chronic difficulties with organization, time management, and emotional regulation can lead to increased stress, anxiety, and other mental health issues. Teens who struggle with these skills may experience lower self-esteem and less satisfaction with life overall.

It's important to note that executive functioning skills aren't fixed traits. They can be developed and strengthened over time with the right support and strategies. That's why understanding these skills is so crucial for parents. By recognizing their importance and actively nurturing them, we can set our teens up for success not just in school, but in all aspects of their lives.

In the next section, we'll explore some of the common challenges teens face when it comes to executive functioning. Understanding these challenges is the first step in helping our teens overcome them.

Common Challenges in Executive Functioning for Teens

If you're nodding along, recognizing your teen in these descriptions, you're not alone. Many teens struggle with executive functioning. Some common challenges include:

1. Procrastination: This is often the most visible sign of executive functioning difficulties. Teens might delay starting assignments until the night before they're due, or put off studying for tests until the last minute. This isn't just about being lazy—it often stems from difficulties with task initiation, time management, and breaking down large tasks into manageable steps.

2. Disorganization: You might notice this in your teen's messy backpack, cluttered desk, or lost assignments. Teens struggling with organization might have trouble keeping track of materials for different classes, managing their school papers, or maintaining a system for storing and retrieving information.

3. Poor time management: This shows up as difficulty estimating how long tasks will take, frequently running late, or struggling to balance multiple responsibilities. Teens might underestimate how long an assignment will take, leading to late nights and rushed work.

4. Difficulty with long-term projects: Projects that require planning and sustained effort over time can be particularly challenging. Teens might procrastinate starting, struggle to break the project into steps, or have trouble pacing themselves to meet deadlines.

5. Trouble following multi-step instructions: You might notice your teen forgetting parts of complex instructions or getting confused when trying to complete tasks with multiple steps.

6. Difficulty transitioning between activities: Some teens struggle to shift gears, whether it's moving from one class to another or switching from homework to dinner time.

7. Emotional dysregulation: This can manifest as overreacting to minor setbacks, having trouble calming down after getting upset, or struggling to maintain a positive attitude when faced with challenges.

8. Impulsivity: This might show up as blurting out answers in class, making decisions without thinking through consequences, or having trouble waiting their turn.

It's important to differentiate between typical teenage behavior and potential executive functioning deficits. Occasional forgetfulness or a messy room? Pretty normal. But chronic disorganization, persistent procrastination, and consistent difficulty managing time? Those might indicate deeper issues.

Consider this real-world example: A high school student consistently struggles with homework deadlines. Despite understanding the material, they can't seem to start assignments until the last minute. This leads to incomplete work, lower grades, and increased anxiety. The underlying issue is often a combination of procrastination and poor time management—classic executive functioning challenges.

Or think about a teen who excels in class discussions but struggles with tests and long-term projects. They might have strong cognitive abilities but difficulty with the executive functioning skills needed to study effectively and manage extended tasks.

Another common scenario is the teen who seems to be constantly forgetting things—permission slips, homework assignments, items needed for after-school activities. While everyone forgets things occasionally, consistent forgetfulness across multiple areas of life can indicate challenges with working memory and organization.

It's also worth noting that executive functioning challenges can sometimes masquerade as behavioral issues. A teen who's constantly interrupting others or having emotional outbursts might be struggling with impulse control and emotional regulation—key executive functioning skills.

Understanding these challenges is crucial because it shifts our perspective. Instead of seeing a lazy or defiant teen, we can recognize a young person who's struggling with specific skills—skills that can be improved with the right support and strategies.

In the next section, we'll explore how to identify these challenges in your own teen. Remember, the goal isn't to diagnose or label, but to understand where your teen might need extra support. With this knowledge, you'll be better equipped to help your teen develop the skills they need to thrive.

Identifying Executive Functioning Deficits in Your Teen

So how can you tell if your teen is struggling with executive functioning? Here are some signs to watch for:

- Consistent forgetfulness (completing assignments, losing items, missing deadlines)
- Difficulty following multi-step instructions
- Frequent emotional outbursts
- Trouble starting or completing tasks
- Chronic disorganization (messy backpack, lost papers, cluttered room)
- Poor time management (always running late, underestimating time needed for tasks)
- Difficulty adapting to changes in routine
- Struggles with long-term projects or studying for tests
- Impulsive behavior or decision-making

If you're noticing these signs, don't panic. There are several ways to assess and address executive functioning deficits:

1. Standardized tests: Tools like the Behavior Rating Inventory of Executive Function (BRIEF) can provide detailed insights. These assessments, usually administered by educational

psychologists, measure various aspects of executive functioning and can help pinpoint specific areas of strength and weakness.

2. Behavioral checklists: These allow you to track specific behaviors over time. For example, you might keep a log of how often your teen forgets homework, loses items, or has difficulty starting tasks. Over time, patterns may emerge that can help identify areas of concern.

3. Professional evaluations: Consulting with school counselors, psychologists, or psychiatrists can provide in-depth assessments. These professionals can conduct comprehensive evaluations, including cognitive tests, behavioral observations, and interviews with you and your teen.

4. Self-reflection exercises: Encourage your teen to reflect on their own experiences. Daily behavior logs, where they track their own challenges and successes, can be illuminating. Questionnaires about daily routines, challenges, and feelings can also provide valuable insights.

5. Open discussions: Have honest, non-judgmental conversations with your teen about their experiences. Ask about what parts of school or daily life they find most challenging, and listen carefully to their responses.

6. Teacher feedback: Teachers often have valuable insights into a student's executive functioning skills. They can observe how your teen manages assignments, participates in class, and interacts with peers.

7. Review of school records: Looking at report cards, progress reports, and teacher comments over time can reveal patterns that might indicate executive functioning challenges.

Remember, identifying these challenges isn't about labeling or diagnosing. It's about understanding where your teen needs support so you can help them develop the skills they need to thrive. The goal is to gather information that can guide your efforts to support your teen's growth and success.

It's also important to consider that executive functioning skills exist on a spectrum. Most teens (and adults!) have some areas of strength and some areas that need work. The key is to identify significant challenges that are impacting your teen's daily life and academic success.

If you do identify significant challenges, consider seeking professional help. School counselors can be a good starting point. They can provide initial guidance and may be able to implement support at school. Educational psychologists or neuropsychologists can provide more in-depth evaluations and specific recommendations. For some teens, underlying conditions like attention deficit hyperactivity disorder (ADHD) may be contributing to executive functioning challenges, and a psychiatrist or psychologist can help determine if this is the case.

Struggles with executive functioning don't define your teen. Many brilliant, successful people have wrestled with these skills. The good news is that executive functioning skills can be improved with the right strategies and support. In the next section, we'll explore how you as a parent can play a crucial role in supporting your teen's executive functioning development.

The Role of Parents in Supporting Executive Functioning

As a parent, you play a crucial role in nurturing your teen's executive functioning skills. While specific techniques and strategies will be covered in detail throughout the book, there are several key qualities and approaches you should embody to effectively support your teen:

1. Provide Consistent Support

Be there to guide your teen through challenges. This doesn't mean doing things for them, but rather offering support as they learn to manage tasks independently. The key is to strike a balance between providing assistance and encouraging autonomy. Be available to offer guidance, answer questions, and provide reassurance, but also allow your teen to take the lead in problem-solving and decision-making.

2. Model Good Behaviors

Demonstrate effective organization, time management, and emotional regulation in your own life. Let your teen see you using strategies to manage your responsibilities and handle stress. Explain your thought processes out loud, showing them how you approach complex tasks or challenging situations. This modeling can be a powerful teaching tool, as teens often learn more from what they see than what they're told.

3. Create a Supportive Environment

Foster an atmosphere that encourages the development of executive functioning skills. This goes beyond physical organization to include emotional and social support. Create an environment where it's safe to make mistakes and learn from them. Encourage open communication about challenges and successes. Ensure that your home is a place where your teen feels comfortable practicing and developing these crucial skills.

4. Take a Collaborative Approach

Engage your teen in joint problem-solving and decision-making processes. Instead of imposing solutions, work together to find strategies that work for them. This collaborative approach helps teens feel more invested in their own development and teaches valuable skills in negotiation, compromise, and self-advocacy. It also shows respect for your teen's growing autonomy and capability.

5. Offer Encouragement and Positive Reinforcement

Celebrate efforts and progress, not just outcomes. Provide specific, constructive feedback that focuses on the process rather than just the result. When offering feedback on areas for improvement, focus on specific behaviors and offer suggestions for next time. This approach helps build confidence and resilience, encouraging your teen to persist in developing their skills even when faced with setbacks.

6. Be Patient and Persistent

Remember that developing executive functioning skills is a long-term process. There will be setbacks and frustrations along the way. Stay positive and keep reinforcing good habits, even when progress seems slow. Your consistent support and encouragement are crucial in helping your teen develop these skills over time.

By embodying these qualities and approaches, you create a foundation for your teen's development of executive functioning skills. Your involvement not only helps your teen navigate current challenges but also sets them up for long-term success and independence. The goal is to gradually shift responsibility to your teen as they develop these crucial skills, preparing them for the increasing demands of adolescence and adulthood.

The Importance of Executive Functioning in the Digital Age

Today's teens face challenges that we never had to deal with. The digital age presents unique hurdles to developing executive functioning skills. Consider:

- Screen time management: The constant temptation of smartphones, tablets, and computers can be a major distraction. Teens might find themselves spending hours scrolling through social media or watching videos when they intended to study. This constant engagement can impede their ability to focus, organize, and manage time effectively.

- Digital distractions and multitasking: The pull to juggle multiple digital activities simultaneously is strong. A teen might be texting friends, watching YouTube videos, and attempting homework all at once. This kind of multitasking can fragment attention and reduce the ability to concentrate on any single activity. Research shows that this constant task-switching can lead to decreased efficiency and increased errors (Madore & Wagner, 2019).
- Information overload: The internet provides instant access to a wealth of information, which can be both a blessing and a curse. Teens might struggle to filter relevant information, leading to overwhelm and difficulty prioritizing what's important.
- Social media impact: While social media offers connection and information, it can also be a major source of distraction and stress. The constant influx of updates and the pressure to stay connected can make it difficult for teens to focus on tasks at hand. Additionally, social media can affect self-esteem and emotional regulation, as teens compare themselves to carefully curated online personas.
- Decreased face-to-face interaction: With more communication happening online, teens might have fewer opportunities to practice important social executive functions in person, like reading social cues or managing conversations.
- Instant gratification culture: The digital world often provides immediate rewards (likes, comments, level-ups in games), which can make it harder for teens to persist with longer-term goals that don't provide instant feedback.

But it's not all doom and gloom. Technology also offers tools that can enhance executive functioning skills. Educational apps and digital planners can help teens improve organization, time management, and focus. For example:

- Task management apps like Todoist or Trello can help teens create to-do lists, set deadlines, and prioritize tasks.
- Digital calendars like Google Calendar can help with scheduling and setting reminders.
- Note-taking apps like Evernote or OneNote can assist with organizing study materials and ideas.
- Focus apps like Forest or Freedom can help teens manage screen time and reduce distractions.
- Mindfulness apps like Headspace or Calm can support emotional regulation and stress management.

The key is finding balance. Here are some strategies to help your teen navigate the digital world while developing crucial executive functioning skills:

1. Set clear boundaries: Establish rules around screen time, including tech-free zones (like the dinner table) and times (like an hour before bed).
2. Model good digital habits: Demonstrate healthy technology use yourself. Put your phone away during family time and talk about how you manage your own digital distractions.
3. Encourage tech breaks: Help your teen build in regular breaks from screens. This could include outdoor activities, reading physical books, or engaging in hands-on hobbies.
4. Teach critical thinking skills: Help your teen learn to evaluate online information critically. This can improve their ability to prioritize and manage information overload.
5. Use technology intentionally: Encourage your teen to use technology as a tool rather than a default activity. Help them choose apps and programs that genuinely support their goals and productivity.
6. Practice digital mindfulness: Teach your teen to be aware of their digital habits. Encourage them to notice how they feel after different online activities and to make conscious choices about their tech use.

7. Prioritize face-to-face connections: While online connections are important, make sure your teen has plenty of opportunities for in-person social interactions to practice important social-emotional skills.
8. Leverage educational technology: Explore digital tools designed to support learning and executive functioning. Many schools use platforms like Google Classroom or Microsoft Teams, which can help with organization and task management.
9. Discuss digital citizenship: Talk with your teen about responsible online behavior, including managing their digital footprint and understanding the permanence of online actions.
10. Be flexible and adapt: As technology evolves, be prepared to adjust your approach. Stay informed about new apps and platforms your teen is using and be open to discussing their benefits and potential drawbacks.

By helping your teen navigate these digital challenges and opportunities, you're not just supporting their current academic success—you're preparing them for a future where strong executive functioning skills will be more crucial than ever.

As we wrap up this chapter, remember: Executive functioning skills are the foundation for your teen's success, both now and in the future. By understanding these skills and supporting their development, you're giving your teen a tremendous gift—the ability to navigate life's challenges with confidence and competence.

This is a journey. There will be ups and downs, progress and setbacks. But with patience, persistence, and the right strategies, you can help your teen develop the executive functioning skills they need to thrive in school and in life.

The digital age may present new challenges, but it also offers unprecedented opportunities for growth and learning. By embracing these opportunities while mindfully managing the challenges, we can help our teens develop into capable, confident adults ready to tackle whatever the future holds.

In the next chapter, we'll focus specifically on strategies for improving focus and attention. Get ready to discover practical tools that can transform your teen's ability to concentrate and get things done. The journey to better executive functioning starts here—and the rewards will last a lifetime.

TWO

Getting Organized

You walk into your teen's room and see a sea of papers scattered across the desk, textbooks piled haphazardly, and a calendar that hasn't been updated in weeks. Sound familiar? This chaos often mirrors the internal disorganization many teens feel. But don't worry —we're about to transform that chaos into order.

In this chapter, we'll explore how a simple tool—the daily planner— can be a game-changer for your teen. We'll dive into strategies for creating effective checklists, breaking down daunting tasks into manageable chunks, and even tackle the challenge of digital organization. By the end, you'll have a toolkit to help your teen master the art of organization, reducing stress and boosting productivity along the way.

Organization isn't just about having a tidy room (though that's certainly a bonus). It's about creating systems that help your teen navigate their busy life with confidence and ease. When teens are organized, they're better equipped to handle the demands of school, extracurricular activities, and social life. They're less likely to forget assignments, miss deadlines, or feel overwhelmed by their responsibilities.

But here's the thing: organization doesn't come naturally to everyone. For many teens, it's a skill that needs to be learned and practiced. And that's where you come in. As a parent, you play a crucial role in helping your teen develop these essential skills. Don't worry if you're not the most organized person yourself—we'll guide you through each step of the process.

Throughout this chapter, we'll share practical strategies, real-life examples, and exercises you can do with your teen. We'll address common challenges and offer solutions that you can tailor to your teen's unique needs and preferences. Remember, there's no one-size-fits-all approach to organization. The key is to find what works for your teen and to be patient as they develop these new habits.

So, are you ready to help your teen conquer chaos and embrace order? Let's dive in!

Creating a Daily Planner for Your Teen

A daily planner isn't just a glorified to-do list—it's a comprehensive system for managing time and tasks. Think of it as your teen's personal assistant, keeping track of everything from homework assignments to social events.

Why is a planner so powerful? For starters, it supercharges productivity. When your teen can see at a glance what needs to be done and when, it becomes easier to allocate time effectively and focus on one task at a time. No more multitasking mayhem!

But the benefits go beyond just getting things done. A well-maintained planner can be a stress-buster, breaking down overwhelming workloads into manageable chunks. It's like having a roadmap for the week —suddenly, that mountain of tasks doesn't seem so insurmountable.

Plus, a planner ensures a balanced life. It's not all about homework and chores; it makes room for fun stuff too. By seeing all their commitments in one place, your teen can strike a healthy balance between work and play.

Now, let's talk about choosing the right planner. It's not one-size-fits-all—the best planner is the one your teen will actually use. Here are some options to consider:

1. Digital apps: Tools like Todoist and Google Calendar are great for tech-savvy teens. They're accessible from any device and often come with handy features like reminders and notifications. If your teen is always glued to their phone, a digital planner might be the way to go.
2. Paper planners: Some teens prefer the tactile experience of writing things down. The act of physically crossing off completed tasks can be incredibly satisfying. Plus, there's no risk of getting distracted by social media notifications when using a paper planner.
3. Bullet journals: For creative types, bullet journals offer a customizable option. Your teen can design a system that fits their specific needs and personality. This method combines planning with artistic expression, which can make organization feel less like a chore and more like a creative outlet.

When setting up the planner, make sure it covers all aspects of your teen's life:

- Academic subjects: Note down homework assignments, project deadlines, and exam dates. Encourage your teen to color-code by subject for easy reference.
- Extracurricular activities: Include sports practices, music lessons, or club meetings. This helps prevent scheduling conflicts and ensures your teen doesn't overcommit.
- Chores and responsibilities: List household tasks to keep your

teen accountable. This teaches valuable life skills and helps them contribute to the family.

- Social events and leisure activities: Because all work and no play... well, you know the rest. Scheduling fun activities gives your teen something to look forward to and helps maintain a healthy work-life balance.

The key to making the planner work? Consistency. Encourage your teen to:

- Conduct daily reviews: A quick check each evening helps them stay on top of tasks and prepares them for the next day. This could become part of their bedtime routine.
- Hold weekly planning sessions: Set aside time each weekend to plan the upcoming week. This is a great opportunity for you to check in with your teen and offer support if needed.
- Incorporate feedback: If something's not working, tweak it. The planner should evolve with your teen's needs. Maybe they realize they need more space for notes, or perhaps they want to add a mood tracker. Be open to adjustments.

Remember, the goal isn't perfection—it's progress. Celebrate the small wins as your teen develops this crucial organizational skill. Did they remember to write down all their assignments this week? That's worth a high five! Did they complete all their tasks for the day? Maybe that earns a small reward.

Here's a practical exercise to get started:

1. Sit down with your teen and create a weekly spread in their planner. Start by filling in fixed commitments like school hours and regular activities. Then, add in homework time, study sessions, and any upcoming deadlines or events. Don't forget to schedule some downtime too!

2. Once you've set up the week, discuss how to use the planner effectively. Show your teen how to prioritize tasks, estimate how long each will take, and schedule accordingly. This is also a great time to talk about the importance of building in buffer time for unexpected tasks or delays.

As your teen gets used to using their planner, you might notice some common challenges. Maybe they forget to check it regularly, or perhaps they struggle to estimate how long tasks will take. These are normal bumps in the road. Work together to find solutions. For example, if they often forget to check their planner, you could set reminders on their phone or leave sticky notes in strategic locations.

Using a planner effectively is a skill that takes time to develop. Be patient with your teen (and yourself!) as you navigate this new system. With consistent use and positive reinforcement, your teen will soon be on their way to becoming a planning pro.

Using Checklists and Templates for Better Organization

Ever feel like your teen is drowning in a sea of tasks? Enter the humble checklist—a simple yet powerful tool for staying afloat.

Checklists are like life rafts in the ocean of responsibilities. They break down big, scary tasks into manageable steps, providing a clear path forward. Each check mark is a mini-victory, boosting confidence and motivation.

Let's say your teen has a science project looming. Without a checklist, it's a vague, daunting monster. But break it down into steps—gather materials, conduct experiments, write the report—and suddenly it's a series of achievable tasks.

Creating effective checklists is an art. Here's how to master it:

1. Categorize tasks: Group similar items together. Academic tasks in one list, personal tasks in another. This helps your

teen focus on one area at a time without feeling overwhelmed by the totality of their responsibilities.

2. Prioritize: Not all tasks are created equal. Teach your teen to identify what's urgent and what can wait. You might introduce them to the Eisenhower Matrix, which categorizes tasks as:
   - Urgent and important (do immediately)
   - Important but not urgent (schedule for later)
   - Urgent but not important (delegate if possible)
   - Neither urgent nor important (eliminate)

3. Set deadlines: A task without a deadline is like a ship without a destination—it'll float aimlessly. Help your teen set realistic deadlines for each item on their checklist.

4. Keep it manageable: Avoid overwhelming lists. Focus on what really needs to get done. A good rule of thumb is to limit daily to-do lists to 3-5 important tasks.

5. Use action verbs: Start each item with a verb to make it clear what needs to be done. For example, "Write introduction for essay" is clearer than "Essay introduction."

6. Break down big tasks: If a task will take more than an hour, break it into smaller subtasks. This makes it less daunting and easier to get started.

Templates are another secret weapon in the organization arsenal. They provide a consistent framework for tackling recurring tasks. Here are some ideas:

- Homework tracking templates: Keep tabs on assignments, due dates, and materials needed. This could include columns for the subject, assignment details, due date, and completion status.
- Project planning templates: Break down big projects into smaller, less intimidating steps. This might include sections for project goals, resources needed, task breakdown, and timeline.

- Daily routine templates: Streamline the day by allocating specific times for study, leisure, and other activities. This helps create structure and ensures important tasks don't fall through the cracks.
- Test preparation templates: Create a structured approach to studying for exams. This could include sections for key topics, practice questions, and areas that need more focus.
- Book report templates: For avid readers or English class assignments, a template can help organize thoughts and ensure all necessary elements are covered.

The beauty of templates is that they're customizable. Encourage your teen to tailor them to their specific needs and preferences. A template for a math whiz might look different from one for a budding artist— and that's okay!

Here's a practical exercise to get your teen started with checklists and templates:

1. Choose an upcoming assignment or project.
2. Sit down with your teen and brainstorm all the steps needed to complete it.
3. Organize these steps into a checklist, grouping related tasks and putting them in a logical order.
4. Add deadlines to each item.
5. Create a template based on this checklist that can be used for similar future assignments.

As your teen uses these tools, they might encounter some challenges. Maybe they struggle to break tasks down into small enough steps, or perhaps they have trouble estimating how long each task will take. These are common issues that improve with practice. Encourage your teen to reflect on what's working and what isn't, and adjust their approach accordingly.

Remember, the goal of checklists and templates isn't to create more work, but to make existing work more manageable. They should simplify life, not complicate it. If your teen finds that a particular checklist or template isn't helping, it's okay to ditch it and try something else.

With consistent use, checklists and templates can become powerful allies in your teen's quest for organization. They provide structure, reduce stress, and give a satisfying sense of progress. Plus, they're skills that will serve your teen well beyond their school years, into college and their future career.

Breaking Down Tasks: The Power of Micro-Goals

Picture this: Your teen is staring at a massive research paper assignment, feeling overwhelmed and unsure where to start. Sound familiar? This is where micro-goals come to the rescue.

Micro-goals are like stepping stones across a rushing river of tasks. Instead of trying to leap across in one bound (and likely falling in), your teen can take small, manageable steps.

Here's why micro-goals are so powerful:

1. They crush procrastination: Big tasks are scary. Small tasks? Not so much. By breaking things down, your teen is more likely to get started. It's much easier to face "write the introduction paragraph" than "write a 10-page paper."
2. They boost motivation: Each completed micro-goal is a win. And wins feel good, spurring your teen on to the next task. This creates a positive feedback loop, where success breeds more success.
3. They build confidence: As your teen checks off micro-goals, they see tangible progress. This reinforces their ability to tackle challenges and builds self-efficacy.

4. They improve focus: Working on small, specific tasks makes it easier to concentrate. Your teen can give their full attention to one manageable piece at a time, rather than feeling scattered by the enormity of the whole project.
5. They reduce overwhelm: Breaking a big task into smaller parts makes it feel less daunting. This can significantly reduce stress and anxiety associated with large projects.

So, how do you implement micro-goals? Let's break it down (see what we did there?):

1. Start by chunking: Take that big assignment and divide it into smaller parts. Research, outline, draft, revise—each becomes its own micro-goal.
2. Set short-term milestones: Instead of "finish the project by Friday," try "complete research by Tuesday, outline by Wednesday," and so on. This creates a clear timeline and helps prevent last-minute rushes.
3. Make it visual: Use a checklist or progress bar to track micro-goals. Seeing progress can be incredibly motivating. You might use a simple to-do list, a project management app, or even a physical chart on the wall.
4. Prioritize: Not all micro-goals are created equal. Help your teen identify which tasks are most crucial and should be tackled first.
5. Estimate time: Encourage your teen to guess how long each micro-goal will take. This helps with time management and gets easier with practice.
6. Build in rewards: Consider setting up small rewards for completing micro-goals. This could be as simple as a short break, a favorite snack, or some screen time.

Let's put this into practice with a common task: writing a research paper.

Instead of one daunting task, it becomes a series of manageable micro-goals:

1. Choose a topic
2. Gather sources (find 5 reliable sources)
3. Take notes on each source
4. Create an outline
5. Write the introduction
6. Write the first body paragraph
7. Write the second body paragraph
8. Write the third body paragraph
9. Write the conclusion
10. Create a bibliography
11. Revise and edit
12. Proofread

Each of these steps is less intimidating than "write a research paper," making it easier for your teen to get started and maintain momentum.

To help your teen start using micro-goals:

1. Choose an upcoming project or assignment.
2. Brainstorm all the steps needed to complete it. Encourage your teen to be as specific as possible.
3. Organize these steps in a logical order.
4. For each step, discuss:
   - How long might this take?
   - What resources are needed?
   - Are there any potential obstacles?
5. Create a timeline for completing each micro-goal.
6. Decide how progress will be tracked (checklist, app, chart, etc.).

As your teen starts working with micro-goals, they might face some challenges. Maybe they struggle to break tasks down small enough, or perhaps they underestimate how long each step will take. These are normal hurdles that get easier with practice. Encourage your teen to reflect on what's working and what isn't, and adjust their approach as needed.

Remember, the goal isn't just to complete the task—it's to build skills and confidence along the way. As your teen masters the art of micro-goals, they'll develop a growth mindset, seeing challenges as opportunities rather than obstacles.

Micro-goals can be applied to all sorts of tasks beyond schoolwork too. Cleaning a messy room becomes less daunting when broken down into "pick up clothes," "organize desk," "vacuum floor," etc. Even personal goals like learning a new skill can benefit from this approach.

By embracing micro-goals, your teen is learning a valuable life skill that will serve them well beyond their school years. They're developing the ability to tackle complex projects, manage their time effectively, and persist in the face of challenges. These are skills that will be invaluable in college, in their future career, and in life in general.

So the next time your teen feels overwhelmed by a big task, remind them: no mountain is climbed in a single leap. It's conquered one step at a time. With micro-goals, they have the tools to start that climb—and reach the summit.

Developing Long-Term Planning Skills

Long-term planning is like charting a course for an epic journey. It's about looking beyond the day-to-day and setting a direction for the future. For teens, this might involve academic goals like improving their GPA or personal goals like learning a new skill.

Developing long-term planning skills is crucial for several reasons:

1. It provides direction: Long-term goals give your teen something to work towards, providing motivation and purpose.
2. It teaches prioritization: When your teen has a clear long-term goal, it's easier to decide what's important and what's not.
3. It builds resilience: Long-term planning involves overcoming obstacles and adapting to changes, which builds important life skills.
4. It prepares for the future: Whether it's college applications or career planning, long-term thinking is essential for future success.

Here's how to help your teen set and achieve long-term goals:

1. Make it SMART: Teach your teen to set Specific, Measurable, Achievable, Relevant, and Time-bound goals. Instead of "do better in math," try "improve math grade from C to B by the end of the semester." For example:
   ◦ Specific: Improve math grade
   ◦ Measurable: From C to B
   ◦ Achievable: Moving up one grade level is realistic
   ◦ Relevant: Better grades align with college admission goals
   ◦ Time-bound: By the end of the semester
2. Create a roadmap: Break the goal down into actionable steps. If the goal is to improve in math, steps might include:
   ◦ Complete all homework on time
   ◦ Attend weekly study sessions
   ◦ Seek help from a tutor once a month
   ◦ Practice extra problems for 30 minutes each day
   ◦ Review notes for 15 minutes after each class
3. Set milestones: These are like checkpoints on the journey. They help track progress and provide opportunities to

celebrate small wins along the way. For our math example, milestones might be:

- ◦ Achieve a B on the next quiz
- ◦ Maintain a B average for a month
- ◦ Improve test scores by 10%

4. Make it visual: Create a timeline or use a goal-tracking app to visualize the path to success. This could be a simple chart on the wall or a digital progress bar. Seeing progress can be incredibly motivating.

5. Review and adjust: Life happens, and plans may need to change. Encourage regular check-ins to review progress and make adjustments as needed. Maybe your teen realizes they need more tutoring than initially thought, or perhaps they're progressing faster than expected and can set more ambitious goals.

Tools for tracking long-term goals:

- Progress journals: Encourage your teen to write regular entries about their achievements and challenges. This not only tracks progress but also promotes self-reflection and problem-solving.
- Tracking apps: Apps like Trello or Asana can help manage goals and deadlines. These tools allow for easy updating and can send reminders to keep your teen on track.
- Vision boards: A visual representation of goals can be a powerful motivator. This could be a physical board with images and words representing their goals, or a digital collage they can set as their computer background.

Long-term planning workshop:

1. Identify a long-term goal: Have your teen choose something they want to achieve in the next 6-12 months.

2. Make it SMART: Work together to refine the goal using the SMART criteria.
3. Create a roadmap: Break the goal down into smaller steps and milestones.
4. Choose a tracking method: Decide how progress will be monitored (journal, app, chart, etc.).
5. Schedule regular check-ins: Set dates for reviewing progress and making adjustments.

As your teen works on their long-term goal, they might encounter some challenges:

- Losing motivation: It's normal for enthusiasm to wane over time. Encourage your teen to reconnect with their 'why' - the reason they set this goal in the first place.
- Unexpected obstacles: Life rarely goes exactly as planned. Help your teen see obstacles as learning opportunities rather than failures.
- Changing priorities: Sometimes, goals that seemed important at first become less so over time. It's okay to reassess and change course if needed.

Remember, developing long-term planning skills is a process. It takes practice, patience, and sometimes a bit of trial and error. But with your support, your teen can learn to set and achieve meaningful goals, building confidence and life skills along the way.

Long-term planning isn't just about achieving specific goals - it's about developing a forward-thinking mindset. As your teen practices these skills, they'll become better at anticipating challenges, seizing opportunities, and shaping their own future.

Decluttering: Strategies for a Clean and Organized Space

A cluttered space often leads to a cluttered mind. Helping your teen create and maintain an organized environment can have a big impact on their focus, productivity, and overall well-being.

Here's why a clean space matters:

1. Improved focus: Less visual distraction means better concentration. When your teen's workspace is clear, their mind can focus on the task at hand rather than being pulled in multiple directions by surrounding clutter.
2. Reduced stress: A tidy environment can help calm a busy mind. Coming home to a neat room can be a relief after a long day at school, rather than another source of stress.
3. Better time management: No more wasting time searching for lost items! When everything has a place, your teen can spend their energy on important tasks rather than hunting for missing homework or that elusive permission slip.
4. Increased productivity: An organized space streamlines work processes. With all necessary materials at hand and distractions minimized, your teen can work more efficiently.
5. Improved sleep: A clutter-free bedroom can contribute to better sleep quality. It's easier to relax and unwind in a tidy space.

So, how do you help your teen declutter? Here's a step-by-step approach:

1. Sort it out: Help your teen go through their belongings, sorting items into three categories: keep, donate, and discard. This can be a big job, so consider tackling one area at a time - start with the desk, then move to the closet, and so on.
2. Organize what's left: Use bins, shelves, and drawers to give everything a home. Label storage areas to make it easy to

remember where things go. Consider using clear containers so items are visible at a glance.

3. Maintain the system: Establish regular clean-up routines. A quick 10-minute tidy at the end of each day can work wonders. Make it a habit - perhaps while listening to a favorite song or podcast to make it more enjoyable.

4. Do periodic purges: Every few months, encourage your teen to reassess their belongings and let go of what they no longer need. This prevents clutter from building up over time.

Creating a dedicated homework station can be a game-changer. Here's how:

1. Choose the right location: Find a quiet spot with good lighting and minimal distractions. This could be a corner of their bedroom, a spot in the family room, or even a converted closet.

2. Stock it with essentials: Pens, paper, calculator, computer— whatever your teen needs for their studies. Keep frequently used items within easy reach.

3. Keep it organized: Use desk organizers, file folders, and other tools to keep supplies tidy and accessible. A pegboard or bulletin board can be great for hanging up schedules, reminders, and inspirational quotes.

4. Minimize distractions: Consider using a white noise machine or noise-canceling headphones to create a focused environment. If the homework station is in a shared space, a folding screen can help create a sense of privacy.

5. Make it personal: Let your teen add some personal touches to make the space feel inviting. This could be artwork, photos, or a small plant.

Kickstart the decluttering process:

1. Choose one area to focus on - let's say the desk.
2. Remove everything from the desk and wipe it clean.
3. Sort through the items, deciding what to keep, donate, or discard.
4. For the items being kept, decide where each one belongs. Does it need to be on the desk, or can it be stored elsewhere?
5. Put things back, with the most frequently used items in easy reach.
6. Maintain the new organization by spending 5 minutes each evening putting things back in their place.

As your teen goes through this process, they might face some challenges:

- Emotional attachment to items: It can be hard to let go of things, even if they're no longer useful. Encourage your teen to consider whether each item truly adds value to their life.
- Feeling overwhelmed: Decluttering can seem like a huge task. Break it down into smaller, manageable chunks - maybe tackle one drawer or shelf at a time.
- Maintaining the new system: Old habits can be hard to break. Gentle reminders and positive reinforcement can help your teen stick to their new organizational habits.

Remember, the goal is to create a space that supports your teen's productivity and well-being. It might take some trial and error to find the perfect setup, but the payoff in improved focus and reduced stress is worth it.

A clutter-free space isn't just about tidiness - it's about creating an environment that supports your teen's goals and reduces unnecessary stress. By helping your teen master the art of decluttering, you're giving them valuable skills that will serve them well throughout their life.

Organizing Digital Files and Schoolwork

In today's digital age, managing electronic files is just as important as organizing physical spaces. A well-organized digital system can save time, reduce stress, and improve efficiency.

Here's why digital organization matters:

1. Quick access to information: No more frantic searching for that one document! With a good system, your teen can find what they need in seconds.
2. Reduced digital clutter: A tidy digital space can be as calming as a tidy physical space. It reduces mental load and makes working on the computer more pleasant.
3. Improved collaboration: Organized files make it easier to share and work with others. This is especially important for group projects or when submitting work to teachers.
4. Better backup and security: When files are organized, it's easier to ensure everything important is backed up properly.

Steps to create a digital filing system:

1. Categorize subjects: Create main folders for each subject or class. For example: Math, English, Science, History, etc.
2. Use subfolders: Within each main folder, create subfolders for assignments, notes, projects, etc. This might look like: Math > Homework Math > Notes Math > Tests Math > Projects
3. Develop a naming convention: Use consistent, descriptive file names. For example: "2023-09-15_History_Essay_Draft1" This system includes the date, subject, type of assignment, and version, making it easy to find and identify files at a glance.

4. Use tags or colors: Many file systems allow for tagging or color-coding. This can be useful for marking priority items or categorizing across subjects (e.g., all essays could be tagged "essay" regardless of subject).

5. Clean up regularly: Just like physical spaces, digital spaces need regular decluttering. Set aside time each week or month to delete unnecessary files and organize new ones.

Useful tools and apps:

- Google Drive: Great for cloud storage and collaboration. It integrates well with Google Docs, Sheets, and Slides, which many schools use.
- OneNote: Excellent for note-taking and organization. It allows for the creation of notebooks, sections, and pages, mimicking a physical notebook structure.
- Evernote: Powerful for tagging and categorizing notes. It's especially good for collecting research from various sources.
- Dropbox: Another cloud storage option that's good for syncing files across devices.
- Notion: A versatile tool that can be used for note-taking, project management, and more. It's highly customizable, which can be great for teens who like to design their own systems.

Maintenance tips:

1. Weekly file reviews: Set aside time each week to organize new files and delete unnecessary ones. This could be part of the weekly planning session we discussed earlier.

2. Regular backups: Use an external hard drive or cloud service to protect against data loss. Teach your teen the importance of backing up their work regularly.

3. Update and evolve: As your teen's needs change, be ready to

adjust the system. What works in freshman year might need tweaking by senior year.

4. Use the search function: Teach your teen how to use file search effectively. Even with the best organization system, sometimes it's faster to search for a file by name.

Here's a practical exercise to get your teen started with digital organization:

1. Choose one subject or project to organize.
2. Create a main folder for that subject.
3. Brainstorm the types of files that will go in this folder (homework, notes, projects, etc.) and create subfolders accordingly.
4. Go through existing files related to this subject and move them into the appropriate subfolders.
5. Rename files as needed to fit the new naming convention.
6. Delete any unnecessary or duplicate files.

As your teen implements their digital organization system, they might encounter some challenges:

- Consistency: It can be tempting to slip back into old habits. Encourage your teen to stick with their new system, even when they're in a hurry.
- Overcomplication: Sometimes, in an effort to be organized, we can create systems that are too complex. If your teen finds they're spending more time organizing than working, it might be time to simplify.
- Digital hoarding: Just like with physical items, it can be hard to delete digital files. Encourage your teen to regularly assess what they truly need to keep.

Remember, the goal is to create a digital organization system that works for your teen. It might take some experimentation to find the right setup, but the result will be a more efficient and less stressful digital life.

By mastering digital organization, your teen is developing skills that will serve them well in college and beyond. In our increasingly digital world, the ability to manage information effectively is a crucial skill for success.

Real-Life Case Study: From Chaos to Order

Meet Emma, a bright high school sophomore struggling with organization. Her room was a whirlwind of crumpled papers and forgotten assignments. Despite her intelligence, Emma's grades were slipping, and her stress levels were sky-high.

When we first met Emma, her parents, Sarah and Tom, were at their wits' end. They knew their daughter was capable of so much more, but her disorganization was holding her back. Emma would often miss deadlines, forget about tests until the last minute, and struggle to find important papers in her messy backpack.

Here's how we helped Emma turn things around:

1. Introduced daily planning: We started by helping Emma choose a planner that suited her style. She opted for a colorful paper planner with plenty of space for notes. We taught her how to use it effectively, scheduling not just homework but also extracurricular activities and downtime.
2. Implemented checklists and templates: We created checklists for common tasks like packing her backpack and preparing for tests. We also developed templates for assignments she frequently encountered, like book reports and math problem sets.
3. Set up a homework station: We designated a quiet corner of Emma's room as her study space. We equipped it with good lighting, comfortable seating, and all the supplies she might

need. Everything had its place, from pens and highlighters to textbooks and notebooks.

4. Developed a digital organization system: Emma learned to categorize and name her digital files consistently. We set up a folder structure in Google Drive that mirrored her school subjects, making it easy to file and find documents.

5. Introduced micro-goals: For larger projects, we taught Emma to break them down into smaller, manageable tasks. This helped her overcome procrastination and made big assignments feel less overwhelming.

The journey wasn't always smooth. We had to adjust strategies along the way:

- We simplified overly detailed checklists that were becoming overwhelming. Emma found that she didn't need to write down every single step; a more general checklist worked better for her.
- We set a specific time each evening for Emma to update her planner. Initially, she would forget to use it, but by tying it to another habit (checking her phone before bed), it became routine.
- We experimented with different digital tools until we found the ones that worked best for her. Emma discovered she preferred Google Drive to Dropbox, and that she loved using the notes app.

The results were remarkable:

- Emma's grades improved significantly. She went from mostly Cs to As and Bs within a semester.
- She became more proactive about starting assignments, often beginning projects well before their due dates.
- Her parents noticed she seemed less stressed and more in

control. The frantic searches for lost papers became a thing of the past.

- Emma's confidence grew as she saw herself succeeding. She started taking on leadership roles in her extracurricular activities, applying the organizational skills she had learned.
- Her teachers commented on the improvement in her work quality and her increased participation in class.

Perhaps most importantly, Emma felt a sense of control over her life that she hadn't experienced before. She was proud of her newfound skills and eager to keep improving.

Emma's story shows that with the right strategies and support, any teen can develop strong organizational skills. It's not about perfection —it's about progress. Emma still has moments of forgetfulness or disorganization, but now she has the tools to get back on track quickly.

For parents reading this, remember that change takes time. Be patient with your teen (and yourself!) as you implement new organizational strategies. Celebrate small victories along the way, and don't get discouraged by setbacks. With consistency and positive reinforcement, you can help your teen transform chaos into order, setting the stage for success in school and beyond.

As we wrap up this chapter, remember that organization is a skill that can be learned and improved over time. With patience, consistency, and the right tools, your teen can transform chaos into order, setting the stage for success in school and beyond.

In the next chapter, we'll explore strategies for effective time management, helping your teen balance schoolwork, extracurriculars, and personal time. Get ready to discover how to make the most of every hour in the day!

THREE

Time Management Techniques

Your teen is juggling school assignments, soccer practice, and social commitments, all while trying to squeeze in some much-needed downtime. It's like watching a circus performer spinning plates—at any moment, one might come crashing down. Sound familiar?

Time management isn't just about getting things done; it's about getting the right things done efficiently. In this chapter, we'll dive into strategies that can help your teen master the art of time management, reducing stress and boosting productivity along the way.

But before we jump in, let's take a moment to consider why time management is so crucial for teens. In today's fast-paced world, teens are under more pressure than ever before. They're expected to excel academically, participate in extracurricular activities, maintain a social life, and possibly even hold down a part-time job. Without effective time management skills, it's all too easy for them to become overwhelmed, stressed, and burnt out.

Moreover, the habits they form now will likely stick with them into adulthood. By helping your teen develop strong time management skills, you're not just setting them up for success in high school—you're equipping them with tools they'll use throughout college, in their future careers, and in their personal lives.

So, are you ready to help your teen transform from a frazzled juggler to a master of time? Let's get started!

Understanding Time Management

Think of time management as your teen's personal superpower. It's not just about completing homework on time—it's about efficiently using time to balance schoolwork, extracurricular activities, social life, and personal interests. When teens master this skill, they can:

1. Efficiently use time: Giving each task the attention it deserves without feeling rushed. This means your teen can focus fully on their math homework without worrying about the English essay they need to write next.
2. Prioritize tasks: Determining which activities are most important and tackling them first. For instance, finishing a project due tomorrow takes precedence over studying for a test next week.
3. Balance multiple responsibilities: Allocating time among various activities without feeling overwhelmed. This could mean dedicating two hours to homework, one hour to soccer practice, and still having time left over for a video chat with friends.

But here's the catch: Even the most well-intentioned plans can go off the rails. Common pitfalls include:

- Underestimating task durations: That "quick" assignment suddenly takes three hours instead of one. This is a common issue for teens who haven't yet developed a realistic sense of how long tasks take.

- Overcommitting to activities: Trying to do it all and ending up burnt out. Many teens, in their enthusiasm, sign up for too many clubs or take on too many responsibilities.
- Lack of prioritization: Spending too much time on less critical tasks, leaving important ones incomplete or rushed. For example, a teen might spend hours perfecting the formatting of an essay while neglecting the content.

These pitfalls can lead to a vicious cycle of stress, procrastination, and poor performance. But don't worry—awareness is the first step to prevention, and we'll cover strategies to avoid these traps.

Mastering time management brings a host of benefits:

1. Reduced stress: When teens manage their time effectively, they're less likely to feel overwhelmed. No more panicked late-night study sessions or frantic rushes to complete assignments.
2. Improved academic performance: With proper time allocation, teens can dedicate appropriate time to studying and assignments. This often leads to better grades and a deeper understanding of the material.
3. More free time: Efficient handling of responsibilities creates space for hobbies and relaxation. Your teen might find they have time for that book they've been wanting to read or that new hobby they've been curious about.
4. Better sleep habits: Good time management often leads to more regular sleep patterns, as late-night cramming sessions become a thing of the past.
5. Increased confidence: As teens see themselves consistently meeting deadlines and achieving goals, their self-confidence grows.

So, how do we assess your teen's current time management skills? Try these methods:

1. Daily activity logs: Encourage your teen to record how they spend their time each day. This can be an eye-opening exercise, revealing where time is being well-spent and where it's being wasted.
2. Self-reflection questionnaires: Ask questions about daily routines and time management challenges. For example: "Do you often feel rushed?" or "How often do you complete assignments at the last minute?"
3. Teacher feedback: Get insights into how your teen manages time in a school setting. Teachers can provide valuable observations about your teen's ability to meet deadlines and stay focused in class.

Here's a practical tool to get started.

Time Management Assessment Worksheet:

1. Daily Activity Log: Record how you spend each hour for one week. Be honest—include everything from classes and homework to social media scrolling and TV watching.
2. Self-Reflection Questions:
    ◦ What activities take up most of your time?
    ◦ Do you feel rushed or stressed while completing tasks?
    ◦ Which tasks do you often leave unfinished?
    ◦ How often do you procrastinate, and on what types of tasks?
    ◦ Do you have a system for prioritizing your work?
3. Teacher Feedback: Ask your teachers about your time management skills. Consider questions like:
    ◦ Do I consistently turn in assignments on time?
    ◦ How well do I manage long-term projects?
    ◦ Do I seem focused and engaged during class?

4. Identifying Improvements: Based on your logs, self-reflection, and teacher feedback, list three areas where you can improve your time management. Set specific, achievable goals for each area.

By using this worksheet, your teen can take an active role in assessing and improving their time management skills. This self-awareness is the first step towards positive change.

Remember, the goal isn't perfection. We're not aiming to turn your teen into a robot, rigidly adhering to a minute-by-minute schedule. Instead, we want to help them develop a flexible, personalized approach to managing their time effectively. This might involve some trial and error, and that's okay. The important thing is to start the process and keep refining it over time.

In the next section, we'll explore a powerful technique that can revolutionize the way your teen approaches tasks and manages their time. Get ready to learn about the Pomodoro Technique!

The Pomodoro Technique for Teens

Ever heard of the Pomodoro Technique? It's like interval training for your brain. Developed by Francesco Cirillo in the late 1980s, this method involves breaking work into focused 25-minute sessions (called "Pomodoros"), separated by short breaks.

Here's why it works:

1. Enhances focus: Short, intense work periods help maintain concentration. It's easier to stay focused when you know a break is coming soon.
2. Reduces burnout: Regular breaks prevent mental fatigue. These short pauses give the brain a chance to rest and recharge.

3. Balances work and rest: Creates a rhythm that keeps your teen productive without feeling overwhelmed. It's like a dance between effort and relaxation.
4. Makes big tasks less daunting: Breaking work into 25-minute chunks makes even the largest projects feel manageable.
5. Helps track productivity: By counting Pomodoros, your teen can see how much time they're actually spending on tasks.

Implementing the Pomodoro Technique is straightforward:

1. Choose a task to focus on. This could be homework, studying for a test, or working on a project.
2. Set a timer for 25 minutes. This is one Pomodoro.
3. Work on the task until the timer rings. During this time, focus solely on the chosen task. No checking phones or social media!
4. Take a 5-minute break. Use this time to stretch, grab a snack, or do something relaxing.
5. After four Pomodoros, take a longer break (15-30 minutes). This extended break helps prevent burnout and keeps your teen refreshed.

The beauty of this technique is its flexibility. Your teen can adjust the intervals based on their needs and attention span. Some might prefer 20-minute work sessions, while others might stretch to 30 minutes. The key is to find a rhythm that works for them.

Here's how your teen might use the Pomodoro Technique for a typical homework session:

- Pomodoro 1 (25 minutes): Start math homework
- 5-minute break: Quick stretch and grab a glass of water
- Pomodoro 2 (25 minutes): Continue math homework
- 5-minute break: Check phone messages
- Pomodoro 3 (25 minutes): Begin English essay

- 5-minute break: Listen to a favorite song
- Pomodoro 4 (25 minutes): Continue English essay
- 30-minute break: Have dinner and relax

Tools to help:

- Pomodoro timer apps (like Tomato Timer or Tide): These apps make it easy to track Pomodoros and breaks.
- Physical timers (yes, even a kitchen timer works!): Some teens might prefer the tactile experience of setting a physical timer.
- Pomodoro logs to track progress: Keeping a log can help your teen see patterns in their productivity and make adjustments as needed.

Here's a simple Pomodoro example log your teen can replicate:

Date	Task	# of Pomodoros	Notes
5/1	Math HW	3	Finished all problems, felt focused
5/1	English Essay	2	Good start, need 2 more Pomodoros to finish

Encouraging your teen to keep a log like this can help them understand their work patterns and improve their time estimates for future tasks.

Some teens might resist the idea of such structured work sessions at first. If this happens, encourage them to try it for just one week. Often, once they experience the benefits—like improved focus and less procrastination—they're more willing to stick with it.

Remember, the Pomodoro Technique isn't meant to be rigid. If your teen is in a great flow state when the timer goes off, it's okay to extend the session. The goal is to create a sustainable work rhythm, not to interrupt productive work unnecessarily.

By breaking work into manageable chunks with regular breaks, your teen can maintain focus, reduce burnout, and achieve a better balance between work and rest. It's a simple yet powerful tool in the time management toolkit.

Breaking Tasks into Manageable Steps

Imagine your teen staring at a massive research paper, feeling overwhelmed before they've even started. Sound familiar? This is where breaking tasks into smaller steps comes in handy.

Why it works:

1. Reduces overwhelm: Transforms daunting projects into a series of achievable actions. Instead of facing a mountain, your teen sees a series of small hills.
2. Increases focus: Allows concentration on one small step at a time. It's easier to focus on "find three sources for the research paper" than "write a 10-page paper."
3. Facilitates progress tracking: Provides visible milestones, boosting motivation. Checking off completed steps gives a sense of accomplishment and momentum.
4. Improves time management: Smaller steps make it easier to estimate how long tasks will take and fit them into available time slots.
5. Enhances quality: By focusing on one step at a time, your teen can give each aspect of the project the attention it deserves.

Here's how to break down tasks effectively:

1. Chunking: Divide larger tasks into smaller, self-contained units. For a research paper, chunks might include research, outlining, writing, and editing.
2. Use checklists: Create a step-by-step list for multi-step

projects. This provides a clear roadmap and the satisfaction of checking off completed items.

3. Set mini-deadlines: Break the overall deadline into smaller, manageable timeframes. This creates a sense of urgency for each step and prevents last-minute rushing.
4. Prioritize steps: Determine which steps are most critical or time-sensitive and tackle those first.
5. Estimate time for each step: This helps with overall time management and scheduling.

Let's apply this to different types of tasks:

Academic projects: For a research paper due in three weeks:

- Week 1: Research and gather sources (2-3 days), Create outline (1-2 days)
- Week 2: Write first draft (3-4 days), Revise and edit (2-3 days)
- Week 3: Write final draft (2-3 days), Proofread and format (1-2 days)

Household chores: Cleaning a messy room:

1. Pick up and put away clothes (15 minutes)
2. Clear and organize desk (20 minutes)
3. Make bed (5 minutes)
4. Vacuum floor (10 minutes)
5. Dust surfaces (10 minutes)

Personal goals: Starting a fitness routine:

1. Research exercises suitable for your fitness level (1 day)
2. Create a weekly workout schedule (30 minutes)
3. Prepare workout clothes and equipment (30 minutes)
4. Start with a 15-minute workout 3 times a week (Week 1)
5. Gradually increase duration and frequency (Weeks 2-4)

6. Track progress and adjust routine as needed (Ongoing)

Remember, flexibility is key. Regularly check in on progress and be ready to adjust the plan if needed. Sometimes, steps might take longer than anticipated or new steps might need to be added. That's okay! The goal is progress, not perfection.

As always, celebrate small victories along the way—they're fuel for motivation! Each completed step is a win and deserves recognition. This could be as simple as a self-high five or a small reward like 10 minutes of video game time.

Here's a practical tool to help your teen break down tasks:

Task Breakdown Worksheet:

1. Task Description: Describe the overall task or project.
2. Final Deadline: When does this need to be completed?
3. Step 1: Identify the first sub-task and set a mini-deadline.
4. Step 2: Identify the second sub-task and set a mini-deadline.
5. Continue until the entire task is broken down.
6. Resources Needed: List any materials, information, or help required for each step.
7. Progress Tracking: Use checkboxes or a progress bar for each step.
8. Adjustments: Note any changes needed and adjust deadlines as necessary.

By using this worksheet, your teen can visualize the breakdown of tasks, making them more manageable and less daunting. It also serves as a central place to track progress and make adjustments as needed.

Encouraging your teen to use this method consistently can lead to improved time management skills, reduced stress, and better project outcomes. It's a valuable skill that will serve them well beyond their school years, into college and their future careers.

Overcoming Procrastination: Practical Tools

Ah, procrastination—the arch-nemesis of productivity. It's the act of delaying or postponing tasks, often to the point where it becomes problematic. Teens frequently struggle with this for various reasons:

- Feeling overwhelmed by the size or complexity of a task
- Lack of clear direction or understanding of how to start
- Fear of failure or perfectionism
- Distractions from technology or social activities
- Low energy or motivation

The impact? Missed deadlines, incomplete assignments, lower grades, and a whole lot of stress. Procrastination can create a vicious cycle where the more a teen puts things off, the more stressed they become, leading to even more procrastination.

But fear not! There are strategies to combat procrastination:

1. The "Eat That Frog" technique: This method, popularized by Brian Tracy, suggests tackling the most challenging task first. It's like ripping off a Band-Aid—once it's done, everything else feels easier in comparison. Why it works:
    - Builds momentum for the rest of the day
    - Eliminates the anxiety of having a big task looming over you
    - Takes advantage of higher energy levels earlier in the day
2. The "Two-Minute Rule": If a task takes two minutes or less, do it immediately. It's amazing how many small tasks we put off that could be quickly knocked out. This rule:
    - Prevents small tasks from piling up
    - Creates a sense of immediate accomplishment
    - Builds the habit of taking immediate action
3. Create a distraction-free environment: Clear the study area of

smartphones, social media notifications, and other attention-grabbers. This might involve:

- Using website blockers during study time
- Putting phones in another room
- Finding a quiet space away from TV or family activity

4. Use positive reinforcement: Reward your teen for completing tasks on time. It could be praise, a small treat, or some extra leisure time. This:

- Associates task completion with positive feelings
- Motivates continued productive behavior
- Acknowledges and celebrates effort and progress

Behavioral strategies can also help:

- Accountability partners: Pair your teen with a friend or family member who checks in on their progress. This adds a social element to task completion and can increase motivation.
- Time-blocking: Set specific time slots for focused work on particular tasks. This creates a sense of structure and can make large tasks feel more manageable.
- Visualization: Encourage your teen to visualize how they'll feel when the task is complete. This can help overcome initial resistance to starting.
- The "5-Second Rule": Coined by Mel Robbins, this involves counting backwards from 5 and then taking immediate action.

And don't forget about tools and apps:

- To-do list apps like Todoist or Wunderlist: These help organize tasks and provide a clear view of what needs to be done.
- Focus apps such as Forest or Focus@Will: These apps can block distracting websites or provide background noise to enhance concentration.

- Habit-tracking apps like Habitica or Streaks: These gamify the process of building good habits and breaking procrastination cycles.

Real-life example: Jake, a high school student, often found himself overwhelmed and cramming at the last minute. Here's how he turned things around:

1. He started using the "Eat That Frog" technique, tackling his most challenging subject (math) first thing after school.
2. Jake used the Forest app to maintain focus, setting it for 25-minute intervals (combining it with the Pomodoro Technique).
3. He found an accountability partner in his friend Sarah. They would check in with each other every evening to ensure they were on track with their tasks.
4. For long-term projects, Jake broke them down into smaller steps and set mini-deadlines for each.

The result? Jake saw a significant improvement in his productivity and a reduction in stress levels. His grades improved, and he found he had more free time to enjoy his hobbies.

Remember, overcoming procrastination is a process. It takes time to build new habits and break old ones. Encourage your teen to be patient with themselves and to keep trying different strategies until they find what works best for them.

Managing Deadlines: Avoiding Last-Minute Rush

Meeting deadlines isn't just about pleasing teachers—it's a life skill that sets the foundation for future success and reduces stress. When teens consistently meet deadlines, they:

- Prevent the vicious cycle of procrastination
- Build confidence and self-esteem
- Create a disciplined routine that serves them well in future academic and professional endeavors
- Reduce stress and anxiety associated with last-minute rushes
- Improve the quality of their work by allowing time for review and revision

Here's a powerful strategy to help your teen stay on track: backward planning.

How it works:

1. Start with the end goal (the deadline)
2. Work backward to identify the steps needed to achieve it
3. Set mini-deadlines for each step

For example, if your teen has a research paper due in four weeks:

- Week 4: Final paper due
- Week 3: Complete final draft, proofread and format
- Week 2: Write first draft, gather feedback
- Week 1: Research and create outline

This approach helps break the project into manageable chunks and ensures steady progress towards the final deadline.

Tools for tracking deadlines:

1. Digital calendars (like Google Calendar):
   - Great for color-coding different types of tasks
   - Can set reminders at various intervals before a deadline
   - Accessible from multiple devices
   - Easy to share with parents or study groups

2. Physical planners or wall calendars:
   - Some teens find writing things down helps reinforce their commitments
   - Provides a visual representation of the month ahead
   - Can be satisfying to physically cross off completed tasks
3. Project management apps (like Trello or Asana):
   - Useful for breaking down larger projects into smaller tasks
   - Can set deadlines for individual components of a project
   - Allows for easy collaboration on group projects
4. Regular check-ins:
   - Encourage your teen to review their calendar at the start and end of each week
   - Use this time to adjust deadlines if needed and plan for the week ahead
   - Celebrate met deadlines and problem-solve for any missed ones

Remember, the goal is to create a proactive approach to managing deadlines, reducing stress, and enhancing academic performance. Here are some additional tips to help your teen master deadline management:

1. Estimate realistically: Many teens underestimate how long tasks will take. Encourage your teen to track how long different types of assignments actually take them, so they can plan more accurately in the future.
2. Build in buffer time: Always plan to finish a day or two before the actual deadline. This allows for unexpected delays or last-minute revisions.
3. Break down larger projects: For big assignments, create a series of smaller deadlines leading up to the final due date.
4. Prioritize tasks: Use techniques like the Eisenhower Matrix to determine which tasks are urgent and important.
5. Communicate with teachers: If your teen is struggling to meet a deadline, encourage them to communicate with their

teacher early. Many teachers appreciate proactive communication and may be willing to grant extensions if asked in advance.

6. Learn from missed deadlines: If your teen does miss a deadline, treat it as a learning opportunity. Help them analyze what went wrong and how they can prevent it in the future.

By implementing these strategies, your teen can develop strong deadline management skills that will serve them well throughout their academic career and beyond.

Balancing School, Work, and Leisure

Finding the right balance between school, work, and leisure is crucial for your teen's overall well-being. It's about:

- Preventing burnout: Constant work without breaks leads to exhaustion and decreased productivity.
- Maintaining mental health: A balanced life helps manage stress and promotes emotional well-being.
- Enhancing productivity: Proper balance actually improves performance in all areas.
- Developing life skills: Learning to balance different aspects of life is a crucial skill for adulthood.
- Fostering personal growth: Time for hobbies and interests contributes to a well-rounded personality.

Here's how to create a balanced schedule:

1. Allocate time blocks for different activities:
   - Schoolwork: Include class time, homework, and study periods.
   - Extracurriculars: Sports practice, club meetings, volunteer work, etc.

- Personal interests: Hobbies, exercise, social time with friends.
- Family time: Meals together, family activities.
- Rest and self-care: Adequate sleep, relaxation time.

2. Prioritize tasks based on importance and urgency:
   - Use techniques like the Eisenhower Matrix to categorize tasks.
   - Ensure high-priority tasks get scheduled first.
   - Be realistic about what can be accomplished in a day.
3. Include downtime and relaxation in the schedule:
   - Schedule specific times for breaks and leisure activities.
   - Encourage activities that promote relaxation and stress relief.
   - Remember that downtime is not just "nice to have"—it's essential for mental health and productivity.

Setting boundaries is key:

- Limit work hours: Set a cut-off time for schoolwork each day.
- Designate study-free zones in the home: Create spaces where your teen can fully relax without thinking about work.
- Learn to say no to overcommitment: Help your teen understand that it's okay to decline some opportunities to maintain balance.
- Establish technology-free times: Implement periods where phones and computers are put away.

Remember to evaluate and adjust regularly. Conduct weekly reviews with your teen to assess how their schedule is working and make necessary adjustments. Ask questions like:

- Did you feel overly stressed or rushed this week?
- Were you able to complete all your important tasks?
- Did you have enough time for relaxation and fun?
- Is there anything you'd like to change for next week?

Here's a sample balanced daily schedule for a teen:

6:30 AM - Wake up, morning routine
7:30 AM - Breakfast and family time
8:00 AM - School
3:00 PM - After-school snack and short break
3:30 PM - Homework and studying
5:30 PM - Sports practice or hobby time
7:00 PM - Dinner and family time
8:00 PM - Free time (social media, TV, reading, etc.)
9:30 PM - Prepare for bed
10:00 PM - Lights out

Of course, this schedule would need to be adapted based on your teen's specific school hours, extracurricular commitments, and family routines. The key is to ensure there's a mix of productive time, social time, family time, and personal downtime each day.

Remember, balance doesn't mean every day has to be perfectly divided. Some days might be heavier on schoolwork, while others might have more time for leisure. The goal is to achieve balance over time, not necessarily within each day.

By helping your teen create and maintain a balanced schedule, you're teaching them valuable life skills and setting them up for long-term success and well-being.

Real-Life Case Study: Mastering Time Management

Meet Maya, a high school junior juggling academics, soccer, and a social life. Her grades were slipping, and stress levels were skyrocketing. Here's how she turned things around:

1. Implemented the Pomodoro Technique: Maya started using 30-minute work intervals followed by 10-minute breaks. This

helped her maintain focus during study sessions and prevented burnout.

2. Broke tasks into manageable steps: Large projects were divided into smaller, less daunting tasks with mini-deadlines. For instance, her history project was broken down into research, outlining, writing, and editing phases, each with its own deadline.
3. Created a balanced schedule: Time blocks were allocated for schoolwork, soccer practice, and relaxation. Maya used Google Calendar to color-code different activities and set reminders.
4. Tackled procrastination: Maya used the "Eat That Frog" technique, tackling challenging tasks first thing after school when her energy was highest.
5. Improved deadline management: She started using backward planning for long-term assignments, ensuring steady progress and avoiding last-minute rushes.
6. Set boundaries: Maya established a "no phone" rule during study times and communicated with friends about her new schedule to manage expectations.
7. Regular check-ins: Every Sunday evening, Maya reviewed her upcoming week with her parents, adjusting her schedule as needed.

The results?

- Improved grades: Maya's GPA increased from a 3.0 to a 3.7 over one semester.
- Reduced stress: She reported feeling more in control and less anxious about her workload.
- Better sleep: By managing her time more effectively, Maya was able to maintain a consistent sleep schedule.
- Improved athletic performance: With reduced academic stress, Maya found she had more energy for soccer practice.

- More quality leisure time: Efficient time management meant Maya could enjoy her free time without guilt or worry about unfinished tasks.

Challenges and adjustments:

- Initially, Maya struggled to stick to her Pomodoro intervals. She adjusted by starting with 20-minute work periods and gradually increasing to 30 minutes.
- She found that some tasks took longer than anticipated. Maya learned to build in buffer time when estimating task duration.
- There were times when social events conflicted with her study schedule. Maya learned to communicate with friends and sometimes say no to maintain balance.

Maya's story shows that with the right strategies and support, significant improvements in time management are possible. It's not about becoming a perfect time manager overnight, but about making consistent small improvements that add up to big changes.

As we wrap up this chapter, remember that mastering time management is a journey, not a destination. It takes practice, patience, and sometimes a bit of trial and error. But with these tools and strategies, your teen can learn to navigate their busy life with confidence and ease.

Encourage your teen to start small—perhaps by implementing just one or two of these strategies at first. As they see improvements, they'll likely be motivated to incorporate more techniques into their routine. And remember, what works for one teen might not work for another. The key is to find a personalized approach that fits your teen's unique needs and personality.

In the next chapter, we'll explore how emotional regulation and stress management play a vital role in supporting teens as they juggle their many responsibilities. Get ready to discover strategies that will help your teen stay calm and focused, even when life gets hectic!

FOUR

Emotional Regulation and Stress Management

Your teen bursts through the front door, slamming it behind them. Without a word, they storm up to their room, leaving a trail of tension in their wake. You've seen this before—the clenched jaw, the furrowed brow, the silence that speaks volumes. When you gently knock and enter their room, you find them buried under blankets, overwhelmed by the day's events.

Sound familiar? This scenario highlights a critical skill many teens struggle with: emotional regulation. It's not just about controlling outbursts; it's about navigating the complex world of feelings in a healthy, productive way. And in today's high-pressure world, it's more important than ever.

In this chapter, we'll dive into the world of emotional regulation and stress management. We'll explore practical strategies to help your teen handle their emotions, cope with stress, and build resilience. By the end, you'll have a toolkit to support your teen in developing these crucial life skills.

Understanding Emotional Regulation

Think of emotional regulation as your teen's internal thermostat. Just as a thermostat helps maintain a comfortable temperature in your home, emotional regulation helps your teen maintain a balanced emotional state. It's not about suppressing feelings, but rather managing and expressing them in healthy ways.

Why is this skill so crucial? Here's why:

1. Mental health: Good emotional regulation is linked to better mental health outcomes. Teens who can manage their emotions are less likely to experience anxiety and depression.
2. Relationship building: When teens can regulate their emotions, they're better equipped to navigate social situations and build strong relationships.
3. Improved problem-solving: Resilience helps teens approach problems with a can-do attitude, rather than feeling defeated.
4. Academic success: Emotional regulation helps teens focus on their studies, even when facing challenges or stress.
5. Future success: These skills lay the groundwork for success in college, careers, and adult relationships.

So, what exactly does emotional regulation involve? Let's break it down:

1. Emotional awareness: This is the ability to recognize and understand one's emotions. It's like being a detective of your own feelings, identifying what triggers certain emotions and how they manifest.
2. Impulse control: This involves the ability to pause before reacting to an emotional trigger. It's that moment of thought between feeling and action.
3. Emotional flexibility: This is the capacity to adapt emotional

responses to different situations. It's about being able to shift gears emotionally when circumstances change.

4. Self-soothing techniques: These are methods to calm the mind and body during stressful or emotional times. Think deep breathing, visualization, or engaging in a calming activity.

Now, you might be wondering, "What's happening in my teen's brain during all this?" Great question! The brain plays a huge role in emotional regulation. Here's a simplified explanation:

- The amygdala: Think of this as the brain's emotional alarm system. It quickly reacts to perceived threats or intense emotions.
- The prefrontal cortex: This is like the brain's wise manager. It helps make decisions, control impulses, and regulate emotions.
- The limbic system: This includes the amygdala and other structures involved in emotional processing and memory formation.

During adolescence, these brain regions are still developing and fine-tuning their connections. This is why teens sometimes struggle with emotional regulation—their brain's "wise manager" is still learning on the job!

Understanding this brain activity can help you appreciate the challenges your teen faces in regulating their emotions. It's not just about willpower; it's about brain development too.

Here's a practical exercise to help your teen build emotional awareness:

Emotion Tracking Worksheet:

1. Emotion: Identify the emotion you're feeling.
2. Trigger: What caused this emotion?
3. Physical sensations: How does this emotion feel in your body?
4. Thoughts: What thoughts are associated with this emotion?
5. Reaction: How did you respond to this emotion?
6. Alternative response: Can you think of a different way to respond?

Encourage your teen to use this worksheet regularly. Over time, they'll start to see patterns in their emotional responses, which is the first step in improving emotional regulation.

Developing emotional regulation skills is a process. It takes time, practice, and patience. In the next section, we'll explore specific techniques for managing stress and anxiety—common challenges that go hand-in-hand with emotional regulation.

Techniques for Managing Stress and Anxiety

Let's face it: being a teen today is stressful. Between academic pressures, social dynamics, and the constant buzz of social media, it's no wonder many teens feel overwhelmed. But here's the good news: there are practical, effective strategies to manage stress and anxiety.

First, let's look at why stress management is so crucial:

1. Academic performance: Chronic stress can significantly impact a teen's ability to focus, learn, and perform well in school.
2. Physical health: Stress isn't just mental—it can manifest

physically too. Headaches, stomachaches, and fatigue are common symptoms of stress in teens.
3. Social relationships: Stress can make teens irritable or withdrawn, straining their relationships with friends and family.
4. Long-term well-being: Learning to manage stress now sets the foundation for a healthier, happier adulthood.

So, what are the common sources of stress for teens? Here's a quick rundown:

- Academic pressures: The expectation to excel in school, get good grades, and prepare for college can be overwhelming.
- Social dynamics: Navigating friendships, dealing with peer pressure, and trying to fit in can be incredibly stressful.
- Family expectations: Pressure from parents to achieve or live up to certain standards can add to a teen's stress load.
- Extracurricular commitments: While beneficial, juggling sports, clubs, and other activities can sometimes feel like too much.

Now, let's dive into some practical strategies to help your teen manage stress and anxiety:

1. Promote a healthy lifestyle: This is the foundation of good stress management. Encourage your teen to:
   - Eat a balanced diet rich in fruits, vegetables, lean proteins, and whole grains.
   - Get 8-10 hours of sleep each night.
   - Stay hydrated by drinking plenty of water throughout the day.
   - Limit caffeine and sugar intake, which can exacerbate anxiety.
2. Teach relaxation techniques: These can be powerful tools for managing stress in the moment. Try:

- Deep breathing exercises: Teach your teen to take slow, deep breaths when feeling stressed.
- Progressive muscle relaxation: This involves tensing and then relaxing different muscle groups in the body.
- Guided imagery: Using imagination to visualize a calm, peaceful place can be very soothing.

3. Encourage physical activity: Exercise is a great stress-buster. It releases endorphins, improves mood, and helps clear the mind. Help your teen find a physical activity they enjoy, whether it's team sports, yoga, dancing, or just taking regular walks.
    - Promote time management: Often, stress comes from feeling overwhelmed by tasks. Continue to reinforce the strategies covered in Chapter 3.

4. Foster a positive mindset: Help your teen reframe negative thoughts into more positive ones. For example, instead of "I'll never understand this math concept," encourage them to think, "This is challenging, but I can figure it out with practice."

5. Create a stress-relief toolkit: Work with your teen to assemble a collection of items that help them relax. This might include:
    - A favorite book or magazine
    - Stress balls or fidget toys
    - Calming music or nature sounds
    - A journal for writing out thoughts and feelings
    - Aromatherapy oils or candles with soothing scents

6. Limit technology use: While social media and smartphones can be fun, they can also be a source of stress. Encourage your teen to take regular breaks from technology and engage in face-to-face interactions or offline activities.

What works for one teen might not work for another. Encourage your teen to try different stress management techniques and find what works best for them. The goal is to build a personalized stress management toolkit they can rely on when things get tough.

Here's a simple exercise to help your teen identify their stress triggers and coping strategies:

Stress Management Worksheet:

1. Stressor: Identify a situation that causes stress.
2. Stress level: Rate the stress level from 1-10.
3. Physical reactions: How does your body respond to this stress?
4. Emotional reactions: What feelings come up?
5. Current coping strategy: How do you usually handle this stress?
6. Alternative strategies: List 3 new ways you could cope with this stress.
7. Action plan: Choose one new strategy to try next time you face this stressor.

By regularly using this worksheet, your teen can become more aware of their stress patterns and develop more effective coping strategies over time.

In the next section, we'll explore how to build emotional resilience—a key skill that helps teens bounce back from challenges and setbacks.

Building Emotional Resilience and Encouraging Positive Self-Talk

Think of emotional resilience as your teen's emotional shock absorbers. Just as shock absorbers help a car navigate bumpy roads, emotional resilience helps your teen navigate life's ups and downs. It's not about avoiding challenges, but about bouncing back from them stronger than before.

We know that emotional resilience promotes better mental health, improves problem solving, enhances relationships, and leads to greater academic success. So, how can we help our teens build this crucial skill? Here are some strategies:

1. Encourage a growth mindset: Teach your teen that abilities and intelligence can be developed through effort, learning, and persistence. This mindset helps them see challenges as opportunities for growth.

2. Foster problem-solving skills: When your teen faces a problem, resist the urge to solve it for them. Instead, guide them through the problem-solving process. Ask questions like, "What are your options?" or "What do you think might happen if you try this?"

3. Promote self-care: Help your teen develop habits that support their physical and emotional well-being. This might include regular exercise, getting enough sleep, or practicing mindfulness.

4. Build a support network: Encourage your teen to cultivate strong relationships with family, friends, and mentors. Having a support system can provide a safety net during tough times.

5. Teach stress management techniques: Equip your teen with tools to manage stress, such as deep breathing exercises, meditation, or journaling.

6. Encourage healthy risk-taking: Support your teen in stepping out of their comfort zone in safe ways. This could be trying a new hobby, speaking up in class, or joining a club.

A crucial component of building resilience is developing positive self-talk. The way we talk to ourselves has a profound impact on how we feel and behave. For many teens, negative self-talk can become a harmful habit, undermining their confidence and resilience.

Here are some strategies to help your teen develop more positive self-talk:

1. Identify negative self-talk: Help your teen become aware of their inner dialogue. Common forms of negative self-talk include:

- All-or-nothing thinking: "If I don't get an A, I'm a total failure."
- Overgeneralization: "I always mess things up."
- Magnification: "This is the worst thing that could ever happen."

2. Challenge negative thoughts: Teach your teen to question their negative self-talk. Are these thoughts realistic? Is there evidence to support them?
3. Reframe negative statements: Help your teen transform negative self-talk into more positive, realistic statements. For example:
   - Instead of "I'm terrible at math," try "Math is challenging, but I can improve with practice."
   - Instead of "Nobody likes me," try "I have some good friends, and I can make more."
4. Use affirmations: Encourage your teen to create and use positive affirmations. These are short, powerful statements that can boost confidence and motivation. For example:
   - "I am capable of handling challenges."
   - "I learn from my mistakes and grow stronger."
   - "I am worthy of love and respect."
5. Practice gratitude: Regularly focusing on things to be thankful for can shift perspective and promote more positive thinking. Encourage your teen to keep a gratitude journal or share one thing they're grateful for each day.

Here's a practical exercise to help your teen transform negative self-talk:

Thought Transformation Worksheet:

1. Situation: Describe a challenging situation.
2. Negative thought: What negative thought came up?
3. Evidence for: What evidence supports this thought?
4. Evidence against: What evidence contradicts this thought?

5. Balanced thought: What's a more balanced, realistic way to think about this situation?
6. Positive affirmation: Create a positive statement to counteract the negative thought.

Changing thought patterns takes time and practice. Encourage your teen to be patient with themselves as they work on developing more positive self-talk.

Coping with Academic Pressure

In today's competitive academic environment, many teens feel overwhelmed by the pressure to excel. While some stress can be motivating, too much can be detrimental to both mental health and academic performance.

Here are some signs that your teen might be struggling with academic pressure:

1. Physical symptoms: Frequent headaches, stomach aches, or fatigue.
2. Sleep changes: Difficulty falling asleep, waking up frequently, or oversleeping.
3. Mood swings: Increased irritability, anxiety, or sadness.
4. Procrastination: Putting off schoolwork more than usual.
5. Perfectionism: Obsessing over grades or being overly self-critical.
6. Loss of interest: Withdrawing from activities they used to enjoy.
7. Declining grades: A sudden drop in academic performance.

If you notice these signs, it's important to address them promptly. Here are some strategies to help your teen manage academic pressure:

1. Teach time management: As we reviewed before, help your teen create a study schedule that allows for balance between schoolwork, extracurriculars, and relaxation. Use tools like planners or digital apps to keep track of assignments and deadlines.
2. Encourage breaks: Regular breaks during study sessions can actually improve focus and retention. The Pomodoro Technique (25 minutes of focused work followed by a 5-minute break) can be particularly effective.
3. Promote a growth mindset: Remind your teen that intelligence and abilities can be developed through effort and learning. This can help them see challenges as opportunities for growth rather than threats.
4. Set realistic goals: Help your teen set achievable academic goals. These should be challenging enough to motivate them, but not so difficult that they feel overwhelmed.
5. Prioritize self-care: Ensure your teen is getting enough sleep, eating well, and exercising regularly. These basic self-care practices can significantly impact both academic performance and stress levels.
6. Teach stress-reduction techniques: Deep breathing, meditation, or yoga can be powerful tools for managing academic stress.
7. Encourage seeking help: If your teen is struggling with a particular subject, encourage them to seek help from teachers, tutors, or study groups.
8. Maintain perspective: Remind your teen that while academics are important, they don't define a person's worth. Encourage them to view setbacks as learning opportunities rather than failures.

Here's a practical exercise to help your teen manage academic stress:

Academic Stress Management Plan:

1. Stressor: Identify a specific academic stressor (e.g., upcoming exam, difficult project).
2. Current feelings: How does this stressor make you feel?
3. Coping strategies: List three healthy ways you can cope with this stress.
4. Action steps: What specific steps can you take to address this stressor?
5. Support system: Who can you turn to for support or help?
6. Self-care plan: How will you take care of yourself while dealing with this stressor?

By regularly using this plan, your teen can develop a proactive approach to managing academic stress.

While it's important to encourage academic success, it's equally crucial to prioritize your teen's mental health and well-being. A balanced approach that values both achievement and emotional wellness will set your teen up for long-term success and happiness.

Developing a Growth Mindset

A growth mindset is the belief that abilities and intelligence can be developed through effort, learning, and persistence. This concept, developed by psychologist Carol Dweck, can be a game-changer for teens struggling with academic pressure and self-doubt.

Here's how a growth mindset differs from a fixed mindset:

Fixed Mindset:

- "I'm not good at math. I'll never understand it."
- "If I fail, it means I'm not smart enough."

- "Why try? I probably won't succeed anyway."

Growth Mindset:

- "Math is challenging, but I can improve with practice."
- "Failures are opportunities to learn and grow."
- "I can achieve my goals if I put in the effort and seek help when needed."

The benefits of a growth mindset are substantial:

1. Increased resilience: Teens with a growth mindset are more likely to persevere in the face of challenges.
2. Improved learning: They're more open to feedback and willing to put in effort to improve.
3. Greater achievement: Research shows that students with a growth mindset often outperform those with a fixed mindset.
4. Enhanced motivation: They're more likely to embrace challenges and stay motivated in the face of setbacks.

Here are some strategies to help your teen develop a growth mindset:

1. Praise effort, not just results: Instead of saying "You're so smart!", try "I'm proud of how hard you worked on that."
2. Encourage embracing challenges: Help your teen see difficult tasks as opportunities to grow, not threats to avoid.
3. Reframe failures: Teach your teen to view failures as learning experiences. Ask, "What can you learn from this?" rather than dwelling on the negative outcome.
4. Promote a love of learning: Encourage curiosity and exploration beyond just getting good grades.
5. Model a growth mindset yourself: Share your own experiences of overcoming challenges and learning new skills.
6. Use growth mindset language: Encourage phrases like "I can't do it yet" instead of "I can't do it."

7. Celebrate progress: Acknowledge improvements, no matter how small, to reinforce the value of effort and perseverance.

Here's a practical exercise to help your teen shift towards a growth mindset:

Mindset Shift Worksheet:

1. Fixed mindset thought: Write down a thought that reflects a fixed mindset.
2. Challenge: How does this thought limit you?
3. Evidence: What evidence do you have that this thought might not be true?
4. Growth mindset alternative: Rewrite the thought from a growth mindset perspective.
5. Action plan: What steps can you take to embrace this new perspective?

Real-Life Case Study: Thriving Under Pressure

Meet Olivia, a high school junior who initially struggled with emotional regulation and academic stress. She would get easily overwhelmed by her workload, leading to emotional outbursts and a sense of helplessness. Her parents, Megan and John, noticed these patterns and sought ways to support her.

They implemented several strategies:

1. Recognizing emotional triggers: They helped Olivia identify situations that caused her to feel overwhelmed.
2. Stress management techniques: Olivia began practicing mindfulness and engaging in regular physical activity.
3. Building emotional intelligence: She started journaling her feelings daily, gaining insights into her emotional patterns.

4. Developing a growth mindset: They encouraged Olivia to view challenges as opportunities for growth.

The journey wasn't without challenges. Olivia initially resisted some techniques, finding them tedious. Her parents adapted their approach, incorporating these practices into her daily routine in more engaging ways.

Over time, Olivia's emotional regulation skills improved significantly. She became more adept at recognizing and managing her triggers, reducing the frequency and intensity of her emotional outbursts. Her ability to handle stress and anxiety also improved, leading to better academic performance and healthier relationships.

Olivia's case highlights the transformative power of targeted strategies for emotional regulation and stress management. It underscores the importance of personalized approaches and the need for patience and flexibility in supporting teens through their emotional challenges.

As we conclude this chapter, remember that developing emotional regulation skills and managing stress is an ongoing process. It requires patience, practice, and support. By implementing these strategies and maintaining a supportive environment, you can help your teen build the resilience and emotional intelligence they need to thrive, not just in academics, but in all aspects of life.

Sharing the Power of Executive Functioning Skills

We have been exploring the critical role of executive functioning skills in teen development and discussing how these skills—including organization, time management, emotional regulation, and decision-making—have become increasingly crucial in our complex, fast-paced world. The digital age presents both challenges and opportunities for developing these skills, reshaping how teens learn, work, and interact with the world around them.

Building executive functioning skills isn't about imposing rigid structures or expecting perfection. It's about helping teens develop the tools they need to navigate their increasingly complex lives, understand their own thought processes, and develop the resilience to push through challenges and setbacks.

I hope that by this stage in your reading, you've seen how the strategies in this book can lead to positive outcomes such as improved academic performance, better stress management, and increased independence. If the insights and activities in this book have made a difference in your approach to supporting your teen's executive functioning development, then you're in the perfect position to help other parents and teens.

By leaving a review on Amazon, you'll help other readers discover the key steps they need to take to support their teens in developing crucial executive functioning skills.

Share your opinion of this book and a little bit about your own experiences applying its strategies. One of the most powerful ways to reinforce your own learning is to help others understand these important concepts.

Thank you for your support. Together, we can highlight the transformative power of understanding and nurturing teen executive functioning skills in our rapidly changing world.

Scan the QR code below to leave your review.

FIVE

Enhancing Focus and Attention

Your teen is sitting at the kitchen table, surrounded by textbooks, notebooks, and a laptop. But instead of diving into their homework, they're staring into space, fidgeting with their pen, or sneaking glances at their phone. Sound familiar?

In today's world of constant distractions, many teens struggle to maintain focus and attention. But don't worry - with the right strategies and understanding, you can help your teen sharpen their concentration skills and boost their productivity.

In this chapter, we'll explore the science behind focus, learn how to create an environment that supports concentration, and discover practical techniques for managing distractions. By the end, you'll have a toolkit to help your teen develop laser-like focus and attention.

Understanding the Science of Focus

Let's start by demystifying what's happening in your teen's brain when they're trying to focus. Think of the brain as a complex orchestra, with different sections working together to create beautiful music - or in this case, sustained attention.

The key players in this focus orchestra are:

1. The prefrontal cortex: This is like the conductor, coordinating all the other parts. It's responsible for decision-making, impulse control, and maintaining attention. When your teen is focusing on a task, their prefrontal cortex is working overtime to filter out distractions and keep them on track.
2. Dopamine: Think of this as the rhythm section, keeping everything moving. This neurotransmitter is crucial for motivation and focus. When dopamine levels are balanced, your teen feels motivated to start and complete tasks.
3. Neural pathways: These are like the sheet music, guiding the flow of information. The more your teen practices focusing, the stronger these pathways become. It's a classic case of "use it or lose it" - the more they exercise their focus muscles, the stronger they get.

Several factors can affect your teen's ability to focus:

- Environmental factors: A noisy or cluttered space can be like static interfering with the brain's focus signal. Just as it's hard to hear a quiet conversation in a noisy room, it's challenging for the brain to focus in a distracting environment.
- Emotional state: Stress or anxiety can drown out the focus orchestra, making it hard to concentrate. When your teen is worried about something, their brain is using energy to process those emotions, leaving less capacity for focusing on tasks.
- Nutrition: The brain needs the right fuel to function optimally. A balanced diet supports better focus. Think of it like putting premium gas in a high-performance car - the right nutrients can help your teen's brain run more efficiently.
- It's also important to be aware of attention disorders like ADHD (Attention-Deficit/Hyperactivity Disorder). If your teen consistently struggles with focus despite your best

efforts, it might be worth consulting a professional for an evaluation. ADHD is characterized by persistent patterns of inattention, hyperactivity, and impulsivity that interfere with daily functioning and development.

If you suspect your teen might have ADHD, it's crucial to seek a professional diagnosis. Treatment options can include behavioral therapy, medication, or a combination of both. Having ADHD doesn't mean your teen can't succeed - many people with ADHD lead successful, fulfilling lives. We'll dive into specific strategies for teens with ADHD in Chapter 8. The key is getting the right support and developing strategies to manage symptoms effectively.

Now, let's look at a practical exercise to help your teen tune into their focus patterns:

Focus Journal:

1. Tasks Completed: List what you managed to finish today.
2. Distractions: Note what pulled your attention away and how you dealt with it.
3. Emotional State: Reflect on your mood and how it affected your focus.
4. Diet and Exercise: Track what you ate and any physical activity.
5. Focus Rating: On a scale of 1-10, how would you rate your overall focus today?
6. Observations: Any patterns or insights you've noticed about your focus?

Encourage your teen to keep this journal for at least a week, then review it together. You might spot patterns that can help you develop targeted strategies for improving focus. For example, you might notice that your teen focuses better after physical activity, or that certain foods seem to boost their concentration.

Understanding the science of focus is the first step in helping your teen improve their concentration. By recognizing the factors that influence focus, you can work together to create an environment and routine that supports better attention and productivity.

Creating a Distraction-Free Environment

Now that we understand what's happening in the brain, let's look at how we can set the stage for better focus. The environment your teen studies in can make a huge difference in their ability to concentrate.

Imagine trying to read a book in the middle of a carnival - that's what it can feel like for your teen to study in a distracting environment. Here's how to create a focus-friendly space:

1. Organize the study space: A cluttered desk can lead to a cluttered mind. Help your teen clear their workspace, keeping only the essentials. This might mean investing in some organizational tools like desk organizers, file folders, or a bulletin board for important notes and reminders.
2. Optimize lighting: Good lighting reduces eye strain and helps maintain alertness. Natural light is best, but a good desk lamp works too. Avoid harsh fluorescent lights that can cause headaches and fatigue. Consider a lamp with adjustable brightness settings so your teen can customize the lighting to their needs.
3. Ensure comfort: An uncomfortable chair can be a constant distraction. Invest in an ergonomic chair if possible. The right chair should support good posture and be adjustable to fit your teen's body. Also, consider the height of the desk - your teen's feet should be flat on the floor and their arms should rest comfortably on the desk surface.
4. Minimize noise: Background noise can be a major focus-killer. Consider noise-canceling headphones or implementing "quiet hours" during study time. If your teen prefers some

background noise, try white noise or instrumental music designed to enhance focus.

5. Create tech-free zones: Designate certain areas of the house as no-phone zones to reduce digital distractions. This could be the study area, the dining room during meals, or the bedroom during sleep hours.

6. Control temperature: A room that's too hot or too cold can be distracting. Aim for a comfortable temperature, typically between 68-72°F (20-22°C).

7. Add some greenery: Studies have shown that plants can improve concentration and productivity. A small potted plant on the desk can make the space more inviting and potentially boost focus.

8. Personalize the space: While you want to minimize distractions, allowing your teen to add a few personal touches can make the space more inviting. This could be a favorite photo, an inspiring quote, or a small memento that motivates them.

Here's a detailed activity to get your teen involved in creating their ideal study space:

Distraction Audit and Action Plan:

1. List all potential distractions in the current study space.
2. Rate each distraction on a scale of 1-10 (1 being minor, 10 being major).
3. For each distraction rated 7 or above: a. Describe why it's distracting b. Brainstorm at least three potential solutions c. Choose the most feasible solution to implement
4. Create an action plan: a. What changes will be made? b. When will these changes be implemented? c. What resources (if any) are needed? d. How will you measure the effectiveness of these changes?

5. Implement the changes and track improvement in focus over two weeks.
6. After two weeks, reassess. What worked well? What needs further adjustment?

What works for one teen might not work for another. Encourage your teen to experiment and find what helps them focus best. Some teens might work well with complete silence, while others might prefer soft background music. Some might prefer a minimalist desk, while others might work better with more personal items around them.

It's also important to note that creating a distraction-free environment isn't a one-time task. It requires ongoing maintenance and adjustment. Encourage your teen to regularly declutter their workspace and reassess what's working and what isn't.

By involving your teen in the process of creating their ideal study environment, you're not only helping them improve their focus but also teaching them valuable skills in self-awareness and problem-solving. These skills will serve them well beyond their academic years, helping them create productive work environments throughout their lives.

Screen Time: Setting Healthy Boundaries

In our digital age, screens are often the biggest hurdle to maintaining focus. While technology can be a valuable tool for learning, unchecked screen time can lead to scattered attention and even digital addiction. The constant notifications, the lure of social media, and the endless entertainment options can make it incredibly difficult for teens to focus on their studies or other important tasks.

Here's why setting boundaries around screen time is crucial:

1. It ensures a balanced lifestyle, making room for other important activities like physical exercise, face-to-face social interactions, and creative pursuits.
2. It promotes better sleep, which is essential for focus and learning. The blue light emitted by screens can interfere with the body's natural sleep-wake cycle.
3. It reduces the constant temptation of digital distractions, allowing for longer periods of sustained focus.
4. It helps prevent digital addiction, which can have serious consequences for mental health and social development.
5. It encourages more mindful and intentional use of technology, rather than mindless scrolling or passive consumption.

So, how much screen time is appropriate? While there's no one-size-fits-all answer, experts generally recommend no more than two hours of recreational screen time per day for teens. This doesn't include time spent on screens for educational purposes or homework. However, it's important to note that even educational screen time should be balanced with offline activities.

Here are some detailed strategies to help manage screen time:

1. Create a family media plan: Set clear rules about when and where screens can be used. Involve your teen in creating this plan to increase buy-in. This plan should cover all family members, not just the teens, as it's important for parents to model healthy screen habits too.
2. Use screen time tracking apps: Apps like Screen Time (for iOS) or Digital Wellbeing (for Android) can help monitor and limit device usage. These apps can provide eye-opening data about how much time is spent on different apps and websites.
3. Establish tech-free zones and times: For example, no phones at the dinner table or in bedrooms after a certain hour. This

not only reduces screen time but also promotes better family communication and sleep hygiene.

4. Implement a 'parking lot' system: Create a designated spot where all family members park their devices during certain hours, like during family time or before bedtime.
5. Encourage alternative activities: Help your teen discover and engage in offline hobbies and activities they enjoy. This could be sports, art, reading, or spending time in nature.
6. Practice the 20-20-20 rule: For every 20 minutes spent looking at a screen, take a 20-second break to look at something 20 feet away. This can help reduce eye strain and provide mini-breaks from screen focus.
7. Model good habits: Remember, your teen is watching you. If you're constantly on your phone, they'll likely follow suit. Make a conscious effort to limit your own screen time and engage in offline activities.

Here's a more detailed template to help you create a family media plan:

Family Media Plan:

1. Screen-Free Zones: (e.g., dining room, bedrooms, car)
2. Screen-Free Times: (e.g., during meals, 1 hour before bedtime, first hour after waking up)
3. Daily Screen Time Limits: a. Weekdays: (e.g., 2 hours of recreational screen time) b. Weekends: (e.g., 3 hours of recreational screen time)
4. Content Guidelines: (What types of content are allowed/not allowed?)
5. Device Curfew: (When do all devices get turned off for the night?)
6. Social Media Rules: (e.g., which platforms are allowed, privacy settings)

1. Consequences for breaking rules: (Be specific and consistent)
2. Rewards for following rules: (Consider non-screen rewards)
3. Family Screen-Free Activities: (List activities you'll do together without screens)
4. Regular Check-ins: (Set a schedule to review and adjust the plan as needed)

By setting clear boundaries around screen time, you're helping your teen develop healthy digital habits that will serve them well into adulthood. Remember, the goal isn't to demonize technology, but to help your teen use it in a way that enhances rather than detracts from their life and focus.

Social Media Distractions: How to Minimize Their Impact

Social media can be particularly challenging when it comes to maintaining focus. The constant stream of notifications, the fear of missing out (FOMO), and the addictive nature of scrolling can all wreak havoc on your teen's attention span. It's important to understand how social media affects focus and what can be done to mitigate its negative impacts.

Here's a deeper look at how social media can impact focus:

1. It creates a cycle of distraction and procrastination: The urge to check social media can interrupt focus every few minutes, making it difficult to concentrate on any task for an extended period.
2. It can lead to comparison and negative emotions: Seeing curated highlights of others' lives can trigger feelings of inadequacy or anxiety, further disrupting focus and emotional well-being.
3. It encourages multitasking: Switching between social media and other tasks can give the illusion of productivity, but actually reduces overall efficiency and the quality of work.

4. It shortens attention span: The rapid-fire nature of social media content can make it harder to focus on longer, more complex tasks.

5. It can be addictive: The dopamine hit from likes and comments can create a cycle of seeking constant validation, making it harder to focus on less immediately rewarding tasks.

To help your teen manage social media distractions, consider these expanded strategies:

1. Set specific times for social media use: Encourage your teen to check social media during designated break times rather than constantly throughout the day. For example, they might allow themselves 15 minutes of social media time after completing an hour of focused work.

2. Use apps to limit access: Tools like Freedom, AppBlock, or built-in phone features can restrict access to social media during study times. Some of these apps allow you to set up recurring schedules, so social media is automatically blocked during designated study hours.

3. Encourage mindful use: Help your teen be more intentional about their social media interactions. Instead of mindless scrolling, they could set specific goals for their social media time, such as connecting with a certain number of friends or finding inspiration for a project.

4. Promote face-to-face interactions: Encourage your teen to connect with friends in person when possible. Real-life social interactions can be more fulfilling and less distracting than digital ones. This could involve joining clubs, participating in sports, or simply hanging out with friends.

5. Practice digital detox: Encourage periodic breaks from social media, such as a "social media-free weekend" once a month. This can help reset habits and reduce dependency on these platforms.

6. Curate the feed: Help your teen clean up their social media feeds by unfollowing or muting accounts that don't add value or that negatively impact their mood or focus.
7. Turn off notifications: Encourage your teen to disable push notifications for social media apps. This can significantly reduce the temptation to check constantly.
8. Use social media blocking extensions: For computer use, browser extensions like StayFocusd or Limit can block social media sites during designated work times.

Here's a reflective exercise to help your teen become more aware of their social media habits:

Social Media Audit and Action Plan:

1. Track social media use for a week: a. Time spent on each platform b. Purpose of each use (e.g., entertainment, communication, information) c. Mood before and after using social media
2. Reflect on the following questions: a. How do you feel when you can't access social media? b. How often do you check social media while doing other tasks? c. How does social media impact your sleep? d. Which social media interactions are most meaningful to you? e. Which ones leave you feeling drained or negative?
3. Identify patterns and areas for improvement: a. What are your most time-consuming platforms? b. When are you most likely to get distracted by social media? c. Which social media habits do you think are unhealthy?
4. Set goals for more mindful social media use: a. Specific times for checking social media b. Platforms you want to use less (or more) c. Types of content you want to engage with more
5. Create an action plan: a. List 3-5 specific changes you want to make b. How will you implement these changes? c. How will you measure success?

6. Implement your plan for two weeks, then reassess: a. What worked well? b. What was challenging? c. How do you feel after making these changes? d. What further adjustments do you want to make?

The goal isn't to eliminate social media entirely, but to help your teen use it in a way that enhances rather than detracts from their life and focus. By becoming more aware of their habits and intentional about their use, teens can learn to harness the benefits of social media while minimizing its potential for distraction.

The Role of Nutrition and Sleep in Focus

You've probably heard the phrase "you are what you eat." When it comes to focus, this couldn't be more true. What your teen puts into their body can have a significant impact on their ability to concentrate. Similarly, the quantity and quality of sleep they get plays a crucial role in their cognitive function and ability to focus.

Let's dive deeper into the nutritional aspect first:

Here are some focus-friendly foods to incorporate into your teen's diet:

1. Nuts and seeds: Packed with omega-3 fatty acids and vitamin E. Walnuts, in particular, are excellent for brain health.
2. Leafy greens: High in folate and vitamins that support cognitive function. Spinach, kale, and collard greens are great options.
3. Whole grains: Provide a steady supply of energy to the brain. They help maintain mental alertness throughout the day.
4. Lean proteins: Help produce neurotransmitters essential for focus. Fish, poultry, and legumes are excellent sources.
5. Eggs: Rich in choline, which is crucial for memory and mental function.

6. Dark chocolate: Contains caffeine and antioxidants that can enhance focus and concentration. Opt for varieties with at least 70% cocoa content.
7. Avocados: High in monounsaturated fats that support brain function and improve blood flow to the brain.
8. Berries: All berries are rich in antioxidants that can improve memory and cognitive function.
9. Green tea: Contains L-theanine, an amino acid that can help improve focus and attention.

Foods to avoid or limit include:

- Sugary snacks and drinks: These can cause energy crashes and negatively impact concentration.
- Highly processed foods: Often lack the nutrients needed for optimal brain function.
- Excessive caffeine: While small amounts can boost focus, too much can lead to jitters and difficulty concentrating.

Now, let's talk about sleep. Just as important as what your teen eats is how much they sleep. Adequate sleep is crucial for focus, memory consolidation, and overall cognitive function. Teens need about 8-10 hours of sleep per night.

Here's why sleep is so important for focus:

1. Memory consolidation: During sleep, the brain processes and stores information learned during the day.
2. Attention restoration: Sleep helps reset the brain's ability to focus and pay attention.
3. Emotional regulation: Lack of sleep can lead to mood swings and irritability, which can interfere with focus.
4. Cognitive performance: Well-rested teens perform better on tasks requiring attention and decision-making.

To promote better sleep:

1. Establish a consistent sleep schedule, even on weekends. This helps regulate the body's internal clock.
2. Create a relaxing bedtime routine. This might include reading a book, taking a warm bath, or practicing gentle stretches.
3. Limit screen time before bed. The blue light emitted by screens can interfere with the production of melatonin, a hormone that regulates sleep.
4. Ensure the bedroom is dark, quiet, and cool. These conditions are optimal for quality sleep.
5. Avoid caffeine in the afternoon and evening, as it can interfere with falling asleep.
6. Encourage regular exercise, but not too close to bedtime. Physical activity can improve sleep quality when done earlier in the day.
7. Consider using a white noise machine or app to create a consistent, soothing background noise.

Here's an expanded version of the sleep and nutrition tracker your teen can use:

Daily Wellness Log:

1. Hours of sleep:
2. Quality of sleep (1-10):
3. Meals and snacks (be specific):
   ◦ Breakfast:
   ◦ Lunch:
   ◦ Dinner:
   ◦ Snacks:
4. Water intake (glasses or ounces):
5. Caffeine intake (type and amount):
6. Physical activity (type and duration):
7. Energy level throughout the day (1-10):

- Morning:
- Afternoon:
- Evening:
8. Focus level throughout the day (1-10):
   - Morning:
   - Afternoon:
   - Evening:
9. Mood (describe):
10. Notable factors affecting sleep or focus:

Encourage your teen to keep this log for at least two weeks. You might notice patterns between their diet, sleep, and ability to focus. For instance, you might find that your teen focuses better after a protein-rich breakfast, or that they struggle to concentrate when they've had less than 8 hours of sleep.

Good nutrition and adequate sleep are foundational to cognitive function and focus. By helping your teen optimize these areas, you're setting them up for success not just in their studies, but in all areas of life.

Real-Life Case Study: Achieving Laser Focus

Meet Alex, a high school junior struggling with focus and falling grades. Despite being bright, Alex was easily distracted, disorganized, and spent too much time on his phone and social media.

When I first met Alex, his parents voiced concerns about his inability to stay focused. His room was a mess, his study habits were inconsistent, and he often seemed overwhelmed by his workload. It was clear that Alex needed a structured plan to regain his focus and improve his academic performance.

Here's how we helped Alex improve his focus:

1. Created a distraction-free study space: We started by decluttering Alex's desk, ensuring that only essential study materials remained. We added proper lighting with an adjustable desk lamp and invested in a comfortable, ergonomic chair. This clean, organized environment helped Alex feel more in control and less overwhelmed by his tasks.

2. Implemented screen time limits: We used tracking apps to monitor and limit Alex's device usage, especially during study hours. We set up specific times for checking social media and messages, rather than allowing constant access.

3. Established a consistent routine: We created a daily schedule that included dedicated study times, breaks, and a consistent sleep schedule. This routine helped Alex's brain know when it was time to focus on work and when it was time to relax.

4. Improved nutrition: We worked with Alex to incorporate more brain-boosting foods into his diet and reduce sugary snacks. We introduced foods like blueberries, nuts, and leafy greens, and encouraged him to stay hydrated throughout the day.

5. Enhanced sleep habits: We established a bedtime routine that included turning off screens an hour before bed and creating a cool, dark sleeping environment. This helped Alex get the 8-9 hours of sleep he needed to stay focused during the day.

6. Introduced mindfulness techniques: We taught Alex simple meditation and deep breathing exercises to help him refocus when distracted. These techniques proved particularly useful during study sessions and before exams.

7. Broke tasks into manageable chunks: We used the Pomodoro Technique, breaking study sessions into 25-minute focused work periods followed by 5-minute breaks. This helped prevent burnout and maintained Alex's motivation.

The journey wasn't always smooth. Alex initially resisted the changes, especially the limits on his phone use. We adjusted by allowing short, scheduled breaks for checking messages. We also introduced non-screen activities during these breaks, like quick stretches or walks.

Another challenge was maintaining consistency with the new habits. To address this, we created a reward system. For every week Alex stuck to his routine, he earned points that could be exchanged for privileges like extra weekend screen time or a favorite meal.

We also faced setbacks when Alex's motivation dipped after a particularly challenging exam. We used this as an opportunity to revisit his goals and remind him of the progress he'd made. We adjusted his study techniques for that subject, incorporating more visual aids and practice problems.

Over time, the results were remarkable. Alex's focus improved, his grades went up, and he felt more in control of his life. His parents observed that he was less stressed and more engaged in family activities. Alex's teachers also noticed the change, reporting that he was more attentive in class and submitting higher quality work.

Perhaps most importantly, Alex developed a sense of confidence in his ability to manage his time and focus. He started taking on leadership roles in group projects and even began mentoring younger students on study skills.

Reflecting on the journey, Alex shared, "At first, I thought all these changes would be restrictive and no fun. But actually, I feel so much more free now. I get my work done faster and better, and I enjoy my free time without feeling guilty about unfinished assignments."

Alex's parents expressed immense gratitude for the transformation they witnessed. His mother noted, "It's not just about the grades. We've seen Alex grow into a more responsible, confident young man. He's learning skills that will serve him well beyond high school."

Alex's story highlights several key points:

1. The importance of a holistic approach: Improving focus isn't just about willpower. It involves creating the right environment, managing technology use, maintaining good nutrition and sleep habits, and learning techniques to manage attention.
2. The value of consistency and routine: Regular habits help train the brain to focus at the right times.
3. The need for flexibility: What works for one person might not work for another. It's important to be willing to adjust strategies as needed.
4. The power of small changes: Each individual change might seem small, but together they created a significant impact on Alex's life.
5. The long-term benefits: The skills Alex learned didn't just improve his grades; they set him up for success in college and beyond.

This case study demonstrates that with the right strategies and support, any teen can improve their focus and attention. It takes time, consistency, and sometimes trial and error, but the payoff in improved performance and reduced stress is well worth the effort.

As we wrap up this chapter, remember that enhancing focus is an ongoing process. Encourage your teen to keep experimenting with these strategies to find what works best for them. With practice, they'll develop the ability to concentrate deeply - a skill that will serve them well through life.

In the next chapter, we'll explore how to set goals, prioritize tasks, and make effective decisions. These skills build on the foundation of focus we've established here, helping your teen channel their newfound concentration into achieving their dreams.

SIX

Goal Setting, Prioritization, and Decision Making

Your teen is staring at a mountain of homework, extracurricular commitments, and personal goals. They're overwhelmed, unsure where to start, and feeling like they're drowning in responsibilities. Sound familiar?

Don't worry - you're not alone. Many teens struggle with setting goals, prioritizing tasks, and making decisions. But with the right strategies and support, your teen can transform from feeling overwhelmed to feeling empowered and in control.

In this chapter, we'll explore powerful techniques for goal setting, task prioritization, and effective decision-making. By the end, you'll have a toolkit to help your teen navigate their responsibilities with confidence and purpose.

The Importance of Setting SMART Goals

Let's start with a game-changer: SMART goals. This isn't just another acronym - it's a powerful framework that can revolutionize how your teen approaches their objectives.

SMART stands for: **S**pecific, **M**easurable, **A**chievable, **R**elevant, **T**ime-bound

Here's why each element matters:

1. Specific: Vague goals lead to vague results. A specific goal answers the who, what, why, and where. Instead of "I want to do better in school," a specific goal might be "I want to improve my math grade."
2. Measurable: If you can't measure it, you can't manage it. Measurable goals allow your teen to track their progress. "I want to improve my math grade from a B to an A" is measurable and provides a clear target.
3. Achievable: Goals should stretch your teen's abilities but still be within reach. "Study math for one hour daily" is achievable if it fits into their schedule. Unrealistic goals lead to frustration, while achievable ones foster a sense of accomplishment.
4. Relevant: Goals should align with your teen's interests and long-term objectives. Improving a math grade is relevant if it supports their dream of becoming an engineer, for example.
5. Time-bound: Deadlines create urgency and help your teen stay focused. "I want to improve my math grade by the end of the semester" provides a clear timeframe for action.

The benefits of SMART goals are numerous:

- They provide clarity, reducing confusion and helping your teen focus their efforts.
- They increase motivation by allowing your teen to see clear, measurable progress.
- They enable better tracking, making it easier to adjust strategies if needed.

Let's look at some examples of well-defined SMART goals:

Academic goal: "Improve my math grade from a B to an A by the end of the semester by studying for one hour daily and attending weekly tutoring sessions."

Personal goal: "Run a 5K race in three months by following a weekly training plan and gradually increasing my running distance."

Here's how you can help your teen create their own SMART goals:

1. Start by identifying areas for improvement. Have an open discussion about what your teen wants to achieve and why it matters to them.
2. Help them make their goals specific and measurable. Ask questions like "How will you know when you've achieved this goal?"
3. Ensure the goals are achievable. Consider your teen's current abilities and resources. The goal should be challenging but not impossible.
4. Check that the goals are relevant to your teen's interests and long-term aspirations. This alignment keeps them engaged and motivated.
5. Set clear timelines. Break down larger goals into smaller, time-bound milestones.

Remember, goal-setting is a skill that improves with practice. Encourage your teen to regularly review and adjust their goals, celebrating progress along the way.

Here's a practical exercise to get started:

SMART Goal Workshop:

1. Choose one academic and one personal goal.
2. Use the SMART framework to refine each goal.
3. Write down the goals and the steps needed to achieve them.

4. Create a timeline for each goal, including milestones.
5. Schedule regular check-ins to review progress and make adjustments.

By guiding your teen through this process, you're equipping them with a powerful tool for achieving success. SMART goals provide a clear roadmap, keeping them focused, motivated, and on track to reach their full potential.

In the next section, we'll explore how to prioritize tasks effectively, ensuring your teen can manage their time and energy efficiently as they work towards their goals.

Prioritizing Tasks Effectively

Now that your teen has set SMART goals, the next challenge is managing the day-to-day tasks that will lead them to success. This is where prioritization comes in.

Imagine your teen's to-do list as a jumbled puzzle. Prioritization is the process of sorting those pieces, figuring out which ones are crucial and which can wait. It's about making smart choices with limited time and energy.

Why is prioritization so important? Here's why:

1. It prevents overwhelm: A long, unorganized list of tasks can be paralyzing. Prioritization breaks it down into manageable chunks.
2. It boosts productivity: By focusing on what's truly important, your teen can make significant progress on their goals.
3. It reduces stress: Knowing what needs to be done and when can alleviate anxiety about missed deadlines or forgotten tasks.
4. It helps with time management: Prioritization ensures that time is spent on high-impact activities rather than busy work.

Let's explore some effective prioritization strategies:

The Eisenhower Matrix

This powerful tool, named after President Dwight D. Eisenhower, helps categorize tasks based on their urgency and importance. Here's how it works:

1. Urgent and Important: Do these tasks immediately. Examples: Finishing a project due tomorrow, studying for a test next morning.
2. Important but Not Urgent: Schedule these for later. Examples: Long-term project planning, regular study sessions.
3. Urgent but Not Important: Delegate if possible. Examples: Some emails, certain meetings.
4. Neither Urgent nor Important: Eliminate these. Examples: Excessive social media scrolling, binge-watching TV shows.

Encourage your teen to use this matrix when planning their week or day. It can be eye-opening to see where their time is really going.

Creating Daily Task Lists

Help your teen start each day with a prioritized task list. Here's a simple method:

1. List all tasks for the day.
2. Categorize each task as high, medium, or low priority.
3. Assign specific time slots to high-priority tasks.
4. Fit medium-priority tasks around these.
5. Low-priority tasks get done if there's time left over.

Remember, flexibility is key. New tasks may arise, and priorities might shift. Teach your teen to reassess their list throughout the day and adjust as needed.

Here's a practical exercise to help your teen get started with prioritization:

Task Prioritization Workshop:

1. List all tasks and commitments for the coming week.
2. Use the Eisenhower Matrix to categorize each task.
3. Create a daily schedule, allocating time for high-priority tasks first.
4. Identify tasks that can be delegated or eliminated.
5. At the end of each day, review and adjust the next day's plan.

By mastering prioritization, your teen will learn to focus on what truly matters, making steady progress towards their goals while managing their daily responsibilities effectively.

Using Visual Aids to Track Progress

Now that your teen has set SMART goals and learned to prioritize tasks, it's time to talk about tracking progress. This is where visual aids come in handy.

Why are visual aids so powerful? Because they provide a tangible representation of progress. They're like a map, showing your teen how far they've come and how far they have left to go. This visual feedback can be incredibly motivating, especially when the journey towards a goal feels long or challenging.

Let's explore some effective visual aids:

Progress Charts

These are simple yet powerful tools. A progress chart could be a bar graph showing grades over time, or a line chart tracking study hours. The key is to make it visually appealing and easy to update.

For example, if your teen's goal is to improve their math grade, they could create a chart with test scores on the y-axis and dates on the x-axis. Each new test score gets plotted, creating a visual representation of their progress.

Vision Boards

A vision board is a collage of images and words that represent your teen's goals and aspirations. It's a creative way to keep goals front and center.

To create a vision board:

1. Gather magazines, printouts, photos, and inspirational quotes.
2. Choose a large poster board or cork board.
3. Have your teen select images and words that represent their goals.
4. Arrange and glue these elements onto the board.
5. Display the board where your teen will see it daily.

Task Boards

Inspired by project management techniques, task boards help visualize workflow. They typically have columns like "To Do," "In Progress," and "Done."

Your teen can create a task board using a whiteboard, bulletin board, or even a digital tool like Trello. As tasks move from left to right, your teen gets a visual sense of progress and accomplishment.

Digital Tools

In our tech-savvy world, don't overlook digital tools for tracking progress. Apps like Habitica turn goal-tracking into a game, while tools like Google Calendar can help visualize how time is spent.

Here's a fun activity to get your teen started with visual aids:

Progress Tracking Art Project:

1. Choose a goal to track visually.
2. Decide on a visual representation (chart, board, digital tool, etc.).
3. Gather necessary materials.
4. Create the visual aid together, making it colorful and personalized.
5. Determine how and when progress will be updated.
6. Display the visual aid prominently.

Remember, the best visual aid is one that resonates with your teen. Encourage them to get creative and find a method that feels inspiring and fun to use.

By incorporating visual aids into their goal-tracking process, your teen can stay motivated, celebrate progress, and maintain focus on their objectives. It's a powerful way to turn abstract goals into concrete, visible achievements.

Balancing Short-Term and Long-Term Goals

Imagine your teen is juggling several balls - some represent immediate tasks, others represent future aspirations. The trick is to keep all of these balls in the air without dropping any. This is the essence of balancing short-term and long-term goals.

Short-term goals are the stepping stones that lead to long-term success. They're the daily and weekly tasks that, when accomplished consistently, pave the way to bigger achievements. Long-term goals, on the other hand, are the big picture aspirations that give direction and purpose to these daily efforts.

Here's why understanding this balance is crucial:

1. It provides motivation: Short-term goals offer quick wins that keep your teen motivated, while long-term goals provide the overarching purpose.
2. It develops time management skills: Balancing both types of goals teaches your teen to manage their time effectively across different timescales.
3. It builds resilience: Working towards long-term goals while managing short-term tasks develops perseverance and adaptability.
4. It enhances decision-making: Understanding how short-term actions impact long-term outcomes improves your teen's ability to make wise choices.

Let's look at some strategies for creating this balance:

Setting Milestones

Milestones are like checkpoints on the road to a long-term goal. They break down the journey into manageable segments. For example, if your teen's long-term goal is to get into a prestigious university, milestones might include:

- Achieving a certain GPA each semester
- Scoring target points on standardized tests
- Completing a certain number of community service hours
- Securing leadership positions in extracurricular activities

By focusing on these milestones, your teen can see tangible progress towards their long-term goal while managing short-term tasks.

Aligning Daily Actions with Long-Term Vision

Help your teen see how their daily activities contribute to their long-term goals. For instance:

- Daily math practice (short-term) supports the goal of improving their math grade (medium-term), which contributes to their dream of becoming an engineer (long-term).
- Weekly soccer practice (short-term) builds skills for winning matches (medium-term), potentially leading to a college sports scholarship (long-term).

This alignment gives purpose to daily tasks and keeps your teen motivated even when the work gets challenging.

Regular Review and Adjustment

Goals aren't set in stone. Life changes, new opportunities arise, and priorities shift. Encourage your teen to regularly review and adjust their goals. Here's a simple process:

1. Monthly Check-in: Review progress on short-term goals and how they're contributing to long-term objectives.
2. Quarterly Assessment: Evaluate overall progress, celebrate achievements, and identify areas for improvement.
3. Annual Review: Reassess long-term goals, set new short-term objectives, and make any necessary adjustments to the overall plan.

This flexibility ensures that your teen's goals remain relevant and achievable as they grow and change.

Here's a practical exercise to help your teen balance their goals:

Goal Balancing Workshop:

1. List all current short-term and long-term goals.
2. For each long-term goal, identify 3-5 short-term actions that support it.
3. Create a timeline that includes both short-term tasks and long-term milestones.
4. Discuss how daily and weekly activities align with long-term aspirations.
5. Schedule monthly, quarterly, and annual review sessions.

By mastering this balance, your teen will develop a strategic mindset that serves them well in school, future careers, and life in general.

Staying Motivated and Overcoming Setbacks

The path to achieving goals is rarely a straight line. There will be ups and downs, moments of triumph and times of frustration. The key to success lies in staying motivated through it all and bouncing back from setbacks.

Why is motivation so crucial? It's the fuel that keeps your teen moving towards their goals, even when the going gets tough. It's what gets them out of bed to study, practice, or work on their projects. Without motivation, even the best-laid plans can fall apart.

Let's explore some strategies to keep that motivational fire burning:

Celebrate Small Wins

Every step forward, no matter how small, is progress. Encourage your teen to celebrate these small victories:

- Completing a challenging homework assignment

- Sticking to a study schedule for a week
- Improving a test score, even if it's just by a few points

These celebrations reinforce positive behaviors and provide a motivational boost.

Visualize Success

Visualization is a powerful tool used by athletes, entrepreneurs, and high achievers in every field. Encourage your teen to spend a few minutes each day visualizing themselves achieving their goals:

- What does success look like?
- How does it feel?
- What steps did they take to get there?

This mental rehearsal can boost confidence and motivation.

Use a Motivation Journal

A motivation journal can be a powerful tool for maintaining focus and enthusiasm. Encourage your teen to write in their journal daily, addressing prompts like:

- What are you grateful for today?
- What progress did you make towards your goals?
- What challenges did you overcome?
- What are you looking forward to tomorrow?

This practice keeps goals front and center and helps maintain a positive mindset.

Create a Support Network

Surrounding yourself with supportive people can make a huge difference in staying motivated. Encourage your teen to:

- Share their goals with friends and family who will cheer them on
- Find a study buddy or accountability partner
- Join clubs or groups related to their interests and goals

Having people to share the journey with can provide encouragement, advice, and motivation.

Now, let's talk about overcoming setbacks. Setbacks are a normal part of any journey towards a goal. The key is not to avoid them (which is impossible) but to learn how to bounce back from them. Here are some strategies:

Reframe Failures as Learning Opportunities

Help your teen see setbacks not as failures, but as valuable lessons. Ask questions like:

- What can you learn from this experience?
- How can you use this knowledge to improve next time?
- What would you do differently if you could do it over?

This reframing turns negative experiences into stepping stones for growth.

Adjust Goals Without Giving Up

Sometimes, setbacks mean it's time to adjust goals. This isn't giving up - it's being flexible and realistic. If your teen is struggling to meet a goal, help them:

- Break it down into smaller, more manageable steps
- Extend the timeline if needed
- Modify the goal to better fit their current circumstances

Remember, the aim is progress, not perfection.

Seek Inspiration from Others

Share stories of famous people who overcame setbacks on their path to success. For example: Michael Jordan was cut from his high school basketball team before becoming one of the greatest players of all time.

These stories remind us that setbacks are a normal part of any success story.

Here's a practical exercise to help your teen build resilience and stay motivated:

Motivation and Resilience Toolkit:

1. Create a "Wins" jar: Write down small victories on slips of paper and add them to the jar. Review these during tough times for a motivation boost.
2. Design a vision board representing goals and aspirations.
3. Start a motivation journal with daily prompts.
4. List 5 people who can provide support and encouragement.
5. Write a letter to your future self, describing your goals and the steps you're taking to achieve them.
6. Create a "Lessons Learned" document to record insights from setbacks.

By implementing these strategies, your teen can maintain motivation, bounce back from setbacks, and stay on track towards their goals. Remember, it's not about avoiding challenges - it's about developing the resilience to overcome them.

Real-Life Case Study: From Goals to Achievements

Let's meet Clara, a high school sophomore with big dreams but struggling to turn them into reality. Clara wanted to attend a top-tier university, but she often felt overwhelmed by her responsibilities. Her grades were good, but not great, and she struggled to balance her academic work with extracurricular activities and personal interests.

Clara's parents noticed her frustration and decided to help her implement the strategies we've discussed in this chapter. Here's how Clara's journey unfolded:

Setting SMART Goals

Clara and her parents sat down to set SMART goals. Instead of the vague "do better in school," they crafted specific, measurable goals:

1. "Raise my historygrade from a B to an A by the end of the semester by studying for 1 hour daily and attending weekly tutoring sessions."
2. "Join two extracurricular activities and take on a leadership role in at least one by the end of the school year."

These goals gave Clara clear targets to aim for and a roadmap to follow.

Prioritizing Tasks

Clara learned to use the Eisenhower Matrix to prioritize her tasks. She realized she was spending too much time on urgent but unimportant tasks, like responding to every social media notification. By focusing on important tasks first, she found she had more time and energy for what really mattered.

She created a daily task list, categorizing tasks as high, medium, or low priority. This helped her focus on what was truly important each day.

Using Visual Aids

Clara created a vision board with images of her dream university, inspirational quotes, and pictures representing her goals. She hung this in her room where she could see it every day.

She also started using a task board to track her progress on assignments and projects. Moving tasks from "To Do" to "Done" gave her a sense of accomplishment and motivation.

Balancing Short-Term and Long-Term Goals

Clara learned to see how her daily actions contributed to her long-term goals. She set milestones for her long-term goal of attending a top university:

- Achieve a 3.8 GPA by the end of sophomore year
- Score 1400+ on the PSAT by junior year
- Complete 100 hours of community service by senior year

These milestones helped her stay focused on her long-term vision while managing her day-to-day responsibilities.

Staying Motivated and Overcoming Setbacks

Clara faced challenges along the way. She struggled with her first few history tests, despite her increased study time. Instead of giving up, she reframed this setback as a learning opportunity. She analyzed her mistakes, sought extra help from her teacher, and adjusted her study strategies.

To stay motivated, Clara started a "Wins" jar, writing down small victories and reading them when she needed a boost. She also found an accountability partner in her best friend, who shared similar academic goals.

The Outcome

Over the course of the school year, Clara's efforts paid off:

1. She raised her historygrade to an A and improved her overall GPA to 3.7.
2. She joined the debate club and the school newspaper, eventually becoming the editor of the paper.
3. She developed better time management skills, reducing her stress and enjoying her activities more.
4. She felt more confident and in control of her future, with a clear plan for achieving her goals.

Clara's parents noticed a significant change in her attitude. She was more focused, motivated, and proactive about her responsibilities. Clara herself felt a sense of empowerment, knowing she had the tools to tackle challenges and achieve her dreams.

Key Takeaways from Clara's Story

1. SMART goals provide clarity and direction, making big dreams feel achievable.
2. Prioritization helps manage time and energy effectively, focusing on what truly matters.
3. Visual aids serve as constant reminders and motivators, keeping goals at the forefront.
4. Balancing short-term and long-term goals ensures steady progress towards big aspirations.
5. Setbacks are not failures, but opportunities for learning and growth.

6. Consistent effort, coupled with the right strategies, leads to significant improvements over time.

Clara's journey demonstrates that with the right tools and mindset, any teen can transform their goals into achievements. It takes time, effort, and persistence, but the results are worth it.

As we wrap up this chapter, remember that goal-setting, prioritization, and decision-making are skills that improve with practice. Encourage your teen to keep refining these skills, adjusting their strategies as needed, and celebrating their progress along the way.

In the next chapter, we'll explore the crucial topic of parent-teen collaboration. We'll discuss how to communicate effectively with your teen, build trust, and work together towards their goals. This partnership is key to supporting your teen's growth and success, so get ready for some powerful insights and strategies!

SEVEN

Parent-Teen Collaboration

You come home after a long day, eager to connect with your teen. But instead of a warm greeting, you're met with a closed bedroom door and the muffled sound of music. When you finally do see your teen, your attempts at conversation are met with shrugs or one-word answers. Sound familiar?

The teenage years can be a challenging time for both parents and teens. As your child seeks independence, communication can break down, and conflicts can arise. But don't worry - with the right strategies and approach, you can strengthen your bond and navigate these years together successfully.

In this chapter, we'll explore effective communication techniques, collaborative planning strategies, and ways to build trust and accountability. By the end, you'll have a toolkit to help you and your teen work together more effectively, fostering a strong and supportive relationship.

Effective Communication Techniques

At the heart of any strong relationship is good communication. When it comes to teens, this becomes even more crucial. Here are some key techniques to enhance your communication with your teen:

Active Listening

Active listening is about truly hearing and understanding what your teen is saying, rather than just waiting for your turn to speak. Here's how to practice active listening:

1. Give your full attention: Put away your phone, turn off the TV, and focus entirely on your teen.
2. Show you're listening: Use nonverbal cues like nodding and maintaining eye contact to show you're engaged.
3. Reflect back what you hear: Paraphrase what your teen has said to ensure you've understood correctly. For example, "So you're feeling stressed about the upcoming exams?"
4. Avoid interrupting: Let your teen finish their thoughts before responding.
5. Ask clarifying questions: If something isn't clear, ask for more information rather than making assumptions.

The goal is to understand your teen's perspective, not to judge or solve their problems immediately.

Open-Ended Questions

Open-ended questions encourage deeper conversations and help your teen express themselves more fully. Instead of questions that can be answered with a simple "yes" or "no," try questions that invite more detailed responses:

Instead of: "Did you have a good day?" Try: "What was the best part of your day?"

Instead of: "Are you worried about the test?" Try: "How are you feeling about the upcoming test?"

These types of questions show your teen that you're genuinely interested in their thoughts and experiences.

Non-Verbal Communication

Your body language and tone of voice can speak volumes. Pay attention to these non-verbal cues:

1. Body posture: Keep an open posture (uncrossed arms, facing your teen) to show you're receptive to conversation.
2. Eye contact: Maintain appropriate eye contact to show you're engaged, but don't stare, which can feel intimidating.
3. Facial expressions: Be aware of your facial expressions. A furrowed brow might communicate disapproval when you're actually just concentrating.
4. Tone of voice: Keep your tone calm and neutral, even if the conversation becomes heated.

Empathy and Validation

Showing empathy and validating your teen's feelings is crucial for building trust and encouraging open communication. Here's how:

1. Acknowledge their feelings: Use phrases like "I can see why you'd feel that way" or "That sounds really tough."
2. Avoid dismissing their emotions: Steer clear of phrases like "It's not a big deal" or "You're overreacting."
3. Share similar experiences: If appropriate, share times when you've felt similarly. This can help your teen feel understood and less alone.

4. Offer support: Ask how you can help or simply be there to listen.

Here's a practical exercise to improve your communication skills:

Communication Check-In:

1. For one week, pay close attention to your communication with your teen.
2. After each significant conversation, reflect on these questions:
    - Did I practice active listening?
    - Did I use open-ended questions?
    - Was I aware of my non-verbal communication?
    - Did I show empathy and validate their feelings?
3. Note areas where you did well and areas for improvement.
4. Set a goal to improve one aspect of your communication each week.

Effective communication is a skill that improves with practice. Be patient with yourself and your teen as you work on enhancing your communication.

In the next section, we'll explore how to use these communication skills in collaborative planning and goal-setting with your teen.

Collaborative Planning and Goal Setting

Imagine sitting down with your teen on a Sunday evening, not to lecture or interrogate, but to plan the week ahead together. This collaborative approach can transform how you and your teen tackle challenges and set goals. Let's explore how to make this happen:

Joint Planning Sessions

Regular planning sessions can become a powerful tool for connection and organization. Here's how to make them effective:

1. Set a consistent schedule: Choose a time that works for both of you, perhaps weekly or bi-weekly.
2. Create a comfortable environment: Pick a relaxed setting, like the kitchen table or a cozy corner of the living room.
3. Use the right tools: Have a shared calendar, planner, or digital app ready to use together.
4. Start with a check-in: Begin by asking how your teen is feeling about the upcoming week.
5. Review the previous week: Discuss what went well and what could be improved.
6. Plan for the week ahead: Go through upcoming commitments, deadlines, and goals.

These sessions aren't just about planning - they're about building a partnership with your teen.

Shared Responsibility

Empowering your teen to take ownership of their responsibilities is crucial. Here's how to foster shared responsibility:

1. Divide tasks: Let your teen decide which tasks they'll take on and which you'll handle.
2. Guide, don't dictate: Instead of telling your teen exactly what to do, ask questions that help them figure out solutions.
3. Allow for mistakes: Let your teen experience the natural consequences of their choices (within reason).
4. Celebrate successes: Acknowledge when your teen follows through on their commitments.

Visual Planning Tools

Visual aids can make planning more engaging and effective. Try these tools:

1. Shared digital calendars: Use apps like Google Calendar to keep everyone on the same page.
2. Whiteboard planner: Create a large weekly or monthly planner in a common area.
3. Task board: Use a cork board or app like Trello to track tasks moving from "To Do" to "Done."
4. Goal visualization chart: Create a visual representation of progress towards long-term goals.

Regular Reviews and Feedback

Consistent check-ins help keep plans on track and goals in focus. Here's how to make them effective:

1. Schedule weekly reviews: Set aside time to discuss what worked and what didn't.
2. Focus on improvement: Frame challenges as opportunities to adjust and get better.
3. Provide specific feedback: Instead of general praise or criticism, offer concrete observations.
4. Encourage self-reflection: Ask your teen to assess their own progress and challenges.

Here's a practical exercise to get started with collaborative planning:

Family Planning Workshop:

1. Schedule a time for your first planning session.
2. Gather necessary tools (calendar, planner, whiteboard, etc.).

3. Before the session, ask your teen to think about their goals for the upcoming week/month.
4. During the session:
    ○ Review any existing commitments
    ○ Discuss your teen's goals and how to achieve them
    ○ Plan out the week/month together
    ○ Assign responsibilities
    ○ Set a time for your next review
5. After a few weeks, evaluate how the process is working and adjust as needed.

The goal is to create a system that works for both you and your teen. Be open to adjusting your approach based on what you learn along the way.

Building Trust and Accountability

Trust is the foundation of a strong parent-teen relationship. But trust isn't given - it's earned through consistent actions and open communication. Here's how to build and maintain trust with your teen:

Establishing Trust

1. Keep your promises: Follow through on what you say you'll do, no matter how small.
2. Be consistent: Apply rules and consequences fairly and consistently.
3. Respect privacy: Give your teen appropriate space and privacy.
4. Admit mistakes: When you mess up, own it and apologize sincerely.

Encouraging Open Communication

1. Share your experiences: Open up about your own challenges and how you've faced them.
2. Be transparent about expectations: Clearly communicate your rules and the reasoning behind them.
3. Create a judgment-free zone: Respond calmly to what your teen tells you, even if it's not what you want to hear.
4. Show appreciation for honesty: Thank your teen for being truthful, especially about difficult topics.

Setting Clear Expectations

Consider creating a family contract that outlines:

- Daily responsibilities (chores, homework, etc.)
- Behavioral expectations
- Consequences for not meeting expectations
- Rewards for consistently meeting expectations

Involve your teen in creating this contract to ensure buy-in and understanding.

Being Accountability Partners

1. Regular check-ins: Set up times to discuss progress on goals and responsibilities.
2. Celebrate achievements: Acknowledge when your teen meets their commitments.
3. Problem-solve together: When goals aren't met, work together to understand why and how to improve.
4. Lead by example: Share your own goals and progress with your teen.

Here's an exercise to build trust and accountability:

Trust-Building Activity:

1. Each family member writes down:
   - One way they'll work to build trust this week
   - One goal they want to achieve
2. Share these with each other
3. At the end of the week, discuss:
   - How did everyone do with their trust-building action?
   - What progress was made on goals?
   - What support is needed for the coming week?

Building trust and accountability is an ongoing process. Consistency and open communication are key to success.

Conflict Resolution Strategies

Conflict is a natural part of any relationship, especially during the teen years. The key is not to avoid conflict, but to handle it constructively. Let's explore some effective strategies:

Understanding Conflict Dynamics

First, it's important to recognize common triggers and patterns in your conflicts:

1. Independence vs. control: Teens push for autonomy while parents try to maintain boundaries.
2. Expectations: Misaligned expectations often lead to frustration on both sides.
3. Communication breakdown: Misunderstandings can escalate into full-blown arguments.
4. Emotional intensity: The teenage brain is still developing, leading to heightened emotional reactions.

Identifying these patterns can help you anticipate and defuse potential conflicts.

Effective Conflict Resolution Techniques

1. Active listening during conflicts:
   - Focus on understanding, not on formulating your response.
   - Repeat back what you've heard to ensure you've understood correctly.
2. Use "I" statements: Instead of: "You never listen to me!" Try: "I feel frustrated when I don't feel heard."
3. Find common ground:
   - Look for areas of agreement, even if they're small.
   - Build on these points of agreement to work towards a solution.
4. Brainstorm solutions together:
   - Encourage your teen to suggest solutions.
   - Be open to compromises that respect both your concerns and your teen's need for independence.

Cooling-Off Periods

Sometimes, emotions run too high for productive discussion. In these cases:

1. Establish a time-out signal: Agree on a word or gesture that either of you can use to pause the conversation.
2. Set a cool-down time: Decide how long you'll take before revisiting the issue (e.g., 30 minutes, a few hours).
3. Use the break constructively: Encourage deep breathing, journaling, or other calming activities during this time.
4. Commit to returning to the conversation: Make sure both parties agree to continue the discussion once emotions have settled.

When to Seek Help

Sometimes, conflicts may require outside assistance. Consider mediation or professional help if:

- Arguments become physically or emotionally abusive.
- The same conflicts keep recurring without resolution.
- There's a complete breakdown in communication.
- Either party feels consistently unheard or misunderstood.

Seeking help is a sign of strength, not weakness. It shows you're committed to improving your relationship.

Here's a practical exercise to improve conflict resolution:

Conflict Resolution Worksheet:

1. Describe a recent conflict:
   - What was it about?
   - What triggered it?
   - How did each person react?
2. Analyze the conflict:
   - What emotions were involved?
   - Were there any misunderstandings?
   - What was each person's underlying need or concern?
3. Brainstorm alternative responses:
   - How could each person have communicated more effectively?
   - What compromise might have worked?
4. Create an action plan:
   - What will you do differently next time a similar situation arises?
   - How can you prevent this type of conflict in the future?

Use this worksheet after conflicts to learn and improve your resolution skills over time.

Family Workshops: Learning Together

Family workshops can be a powerful way to strengthen bonds and develop important skills together. They create a shared learning experience that can be both fun and productive. Here's how to make the most of family workshops:

Time Management Workshops

1. Start by discussing why time management is important for everyone in the family.
2. Have each family member list their daily tasks and commitments.
3. Work together to prioritize these tasks using techniques like the Eisenhower Matrix.
4. Create a family schedule, allocating time for work, school, chores, and leisure.
5. Introduce time management tools like calendars or apps that everyone can use.

Organization and Planning Sessions

1. Choose an area to organize together (e.g., a shared living space, study area).
2. Sort items into categories: keep, donate, discard.
3. Create organizational systems together (e.g., labeled bins, color-coding).
4. Develop a maintenance plan to keep the space organized.
5. Apply these principles to personal spaces and schedules.

Emotional Regulation Exercises

1. Discuss common emotions and stressors that family members experience.

2. Introduce techniques like deep breathing, mindfulness, or journaling.
3. Create a "calm corner" in your home with resources for managing emotions.
4. Role-play scenarios to practice using these techniques in real-life situations.
5. Establish a family check-in routine to discuss emotions and stress levels.

Interactive Activities

1. Role-playing: Act out common family scenarios and practice positive communication.
2. Problem-solving games: Use puzzles or team challenges to develop strategic thinking.
3. Trust-building exercises: Try activities that require cooperation and support.
4. Family goal-setting: Create a family vision board or set collective goals.

The key to successful family workshops is to make them engaging and relevant to everyone. Be open to suggestions and adjust your approach based on what works best for your family.

Here's an idea to get you started:

Family Skills Night:

- Choose one evening a week for family skill-building.
- Rotate responsibility for planning the activity each week.
- Activities could include:
  ○ Learning a new skill together (e.g., cooking, basic home repairs)
  ○ Practicing a time management or organization technique
  ○ Doing an emotional regulation exercise
  ○ Playing a cooperative game

- After each session, discuss what you learned and how you can apply it in daily life.

By learning and growing together, you not only develop important skills but also strengthen your family bond. These shared experiences can create lasting memories and a foundation of mutual support and understanding.

Real-Life Case Study: Strengthening the Parent-Teen Bond

Meet the Johnson family: Sarah and Mike, and their 15-year-old son, Alex. Once a close-knit unit, they found themselves drifting apart as Alex entered his teenage years. Communication had broken down, with simple conversations often escalating into arguments. Everyone felt frustrated and misunderstood. Let's see how they turned things around:

Initial Challenges:

1. Communication breakdown: Alex responded to questions with shrugs or one-word answers.
2. Constant conflicts: Disagreements about curfew, homework, and screen time were frequent.
3. Lack of trust: Sarah and Mike felt Alex wasn't being honest about his activities.
4. Resistance to family time: Alex avoided family dinners and outings.

Strategies Implemented:

1. Improved Communication:
   - Sarah and Mike practiced active listening, making a conscious effort not to interrupt Alex.
   - They started using open-ended questions: "What was the

most interesting thing that happened at school today?" instead of "How was school?"

- They acknowledged Alex's feelings without judgment: "It sounds like you're feeling overwhelmed with all your assignments."

2. Joint Planning Sessions:
   - The family instituted a Sunday evening planning session.
   - They used a shared digital calendar to track everyone's commitments.
   - Alex was encouraged to take the lead in planning his week, with guidance from his parents.

3. Building Trust and Accountability:
   - Sarah and Mike were transparent about their expectations and the reasoning behind rules.
   - They created a family contract together, outlining responsibilities and consequences.
   - Regular check-ins were established to discuss progress on goals and any challenges.

4. Conflict Resolution:
   - They implemented a "pause button" technique for heated discussions.
   - Everyone practiced using "I" statements during conflicts.
   - They worked on finding compromises that respected both Alex's growing independence and his parents' concerns.

5. Family Workshops:
   - Monthly family skill nights were introduced, rotating responsibility for planning.
   - They tackled topics like time management, organization, and stress reduction together.

Challenges Faced:

1. Initial resistance: Alex was skeptical about the new approaches at first.
2. Consistency: It was challenging for everyone to stick to the new habits, especially during busy or stressful times.
3. Old patterns: Sometimes, they fell back into old communication patterns during conflicts.
4. Balancing independence: Finding the right balance between guidance and autonomy was an ongoing process.

Adjustments Made:

1. Flexibility: They adjusted the timing of family meetings to accommodate everyone's schedules.
2. Personalization: They tailored communication styles to what worked best for Alex (e.g., sometimes texting instead of face-to-face conversations).
3. Patience: They acknowledged that change takes time and celebrated small improvements.
4. Feedback loop: Regular family check-ins allowed them to tweak their approach based on what was working.

Positive Outcomes:

1. Improved communication: Alex began to open up more, sharing details about his day and his feelings.
2. Reduced conflicts: Arguments became less frequent and were resolved more constructively.
3. Increased trust: Alex felt more comfortable being honest with his parents, even about mistakes.
4. Better time management: The whole family became more organized and less stressed.
5. Stronger bond: Family time became enjoyable again, with everyone actively participating.

Key Takeaways:

1. Consistency is crucial: Sticking to new habits, even when it's challenging, leads to lasting change.
2. Flexibility matters: Being willing to adjust approaches based on what works keeps everyone engaged.
3. It's a team effort: When everyone participates in creating solutions, buy-in increases.
4. Patience pays off: Change doesn't happen overnight, but persistent effort leads to significant improvements.
5. Communication is key: Open, honest, and empathetic communication forms the foundation of a strong family bond.

The Johnson family's journey demonstrates that with commitment, the right strategies, and a willingness to adapt, it's possible to navigate the challenges of the teenage years and emerge with a stronger, more supportive family dynamic.

Wrapping Up

As we conclude this chapter, remember that strengthening your relationship with your teen is an ongoing process. It requires patience, consistency, and a willingness to adapt. Here are some final thoughts to keep in mind:

1. Keep communication channels open: Even when it's challenging, continue to create opportunities for honest, open dialogue.
2. Lead by example: Model the behavior and communication styles you want to see in your teen.
3. Embrace growth: View challenges as opportunities for both you and your teen to learn and grow.
4. Celebrate progress: Acknowledge and appreciate positive changes, no matter how small.

5. Stay committed: Remember that your efforts to build a strong relationship now will pay dividends for years to come.

By implementing the strategies we've discussed - from effective communication techniques to collaborative planning and conflict resolution - you're laying the groundwork for a strong, lasting bond with your teen. This foundation will not only help you navigate the teenage years more smoothly but will also set the stage for a positive relationship well into adulthood.

In the next chapter, we'll explore specialized strategies for teens with ADD/ADHD, providing additional tools to support teens with unique executive functioning challenges. Whether or not your teen has been diagnosed with ADD/ADHD, these strategies can be valuable for any family looking to enhance focus, organization, and overall executive functioning skills.

EIGHT

Specialized Strategies and Professional Insights

Your teen is staring at their homework, fidgeting with their pencil, and glancing at their phone every few seconds. They've been sitting there for an hour, but barely a word has been written. Sound familiar?

For teens with Attention Deficit Hyperactivity Disorder (ADHD), this scenario is all too common. But don't worry - with the right strategies and support, your teen can overcome these challenges and thrive.

In this chapter, we'll explore specialized techniques for teens with ADHD, insights from school counselors, and ways to leverage technology for better executive functioning. Whether your teen has been diagnosed with ADHD or simply struggles with focus and organization, these strategies can make a world of difference.

Tailored Strategies for Teens with ADD/ADHD

Let's start by understanding what ADHD really means. It's not just about being easily distracted or having too much energy. ADHD is a complex neurodevelopmental disorder that affects how the brain processes information and regulates behavior.

ADHD typically manifests in three main ways:

1. Inattention: Difficulty focusing, easily distracted, forgetful in daily activities.
2. Hyperactivity: Constant motion, fidgeting, talking excessively.
3. Impulsivity: Acting without thinking, interrupting others, making rash decisions.

Some teens may primarily struggle with inattention, while others might be more hyperactive. Many have a combination of these symptoms. It's important to remember that ADHD is not a choice or a result of poor parenting - it's a real neurological difference that requires understanding and support.

Now, let's dive into some strategies tailored for teens with ADHD:

Personalized Learning Plans

One size definitely doesn't fit all when it comes to learning with ADHD. That's where personalized learning plans come in. These plans, often formalized as Individualized Education Programs (IEPs) or 504 Plans, are designed to meet your teen's unique needs.

Here's what they might include:

1. Extended time on tests
2. Breaks during long assignments
3. Preferential seating (e.g., away from distractions)
4. Use of assistive technology
5. Modified homework assignments

The key is to work with your teen's school to create a plan that addresses their specific challenges. For example, if your teen struggles with time management, their plan might include using a digital planner with reminders for assignments and deadlines.

Behavioral Interventions

Behavioral strategies can be incredibly effective for teens with ADHD. Here are some techniques to try:

1. Positive reinforcement: Reward desired behaviors to encourage their repetition. This could be as simple as verbal praise or as structured as a token economy system.
2. Token economy: Create a system where your teen earns tokens for completing tasks or demonstrating good behaviors. These tokens can then be exchanged for rewards.
3. Structured routines: Establish consistent daily routines to provide predictability and reduce anxiety.
4. Break tasks into smaller steps: Help your teen tackle big projects by breaking them down into manageable chunks.

Here's an example of how a token economy might work:

Task	Tokens Earned
Completing homework on time	2 tokens
Organizing backpack	1 token
Following morning routine without reminders	2 tokens

Rewards could include extra screen time, a favorite snack, or saving up for a bigger reward like a new game or outing.

Medication Management

For many teens with ADHD, medication can be a game-changer. There are two main types:

1. Stimulants: These are the most commonly prescribed ADHD medications. They work by increasing dopamine levels in the brain, which can improve focus and reduce hyperactivity.
2. Non-stimulants: These are sometimes used if stimulants aren't effective or cause too many side effects. They work differently but can still help manage ADHD symptoms.

It's crucial to work closely with a healthcare provider to find the right medication and dosage. Every teen is different, and what works for one might not work for another. Regular check-ins with the doctor can help monitor effectiveness and manage any side effects.

Medication is not a magic cure-all. It's most effective when combined with behavioral strategies and environmental support.

Here's a practical exercise to help you and your teen track the effectiveness of ADHD strategies:

ADHD Strategy Tracker:

1. Strategy being used (e.g., token economy, medication, structured routine)
2. Start date
3. Daily rating (1-10) of:
   ◦ Focus
   ◦ Task completion
   ◦ Mood
4. Weekly notes on improvements or challenges
5. Adjustments made
6. Overall effectiveness after one month

Use this tracker to see what's working and what might need adjustment. It can also be helpful information to share with your teen's doctor or school counselor.

By implementing these tailored strategies, you can help your teen manage their ADHD symptoms more effectively. Remember, the goal isn't to "fix" your teen - it's to help them develop the skills and strategies they need to thrive with ADHD.

Behavioral Techniques for Improved Focus

Now that we've covered some general strategies for teens with ADHD, let's dive into specific behavioral techniques that can help improve focus and organization. These methods can be beneficial for all teens, but they're especially powerful for those struggling with attention and executive functioning.

Token Economy Systems

Remember when we mentioned token economies earlier? Let's explore this concept in more depth. A token economy is a type of behavioral modification system that rewards desired behaviors with "tokens" that can be exchanged for privileges or rewards.

Here's how to set up a token economy system:

1. Identify target behaviors: Choose specific behaviors you want to encourage. For example:
   - Completing homework without reminders
   - Staying focused during study time
   - Following morning and bedtime routines
2. Assign token values: Decide how many tokens each behavior is worth. More challenging tasks should earn more tokens.
3. Create a reward menu: Work with your teen to create a list of rewards and their "costs" in tokens. This could include:
   - 30 minutes of extra screen time (5 tokens)

       ◦ Choosing the family movie for movie night (10 tokens)
       ◦ A trip to the ice cream shop (15 tokens)

4. Implement consistently: Be sure to award tokens immediately when the desired behavior occurs.
5. Review and adjust: Regularly review the system with your teen and make adjustments as needed.

The key to a successful token economy is consistency and immediate reinforcement. This system can help your teen see the direct connection between their efforts and positive outcomes.

Self-Monitoring Techniques

Teaching your teen to monitor their own behavior can be a powerful tool for improving focus and organization. Here are some self-monitoring techniques to try:

1. Checklists: Encourage your teen to create daily or weekly checklists of tasks they need to complete. The act of checking off completed items can be very satisfying and motivating.
2. Self-assessment forms: Have your teen rate their focus and productivity at the end of each study session or school day. This can help them become more aware of their habits and patterns.
3. Time tracking: Teach your teen to estimate how long tasks will take and then track the actual time spent. This can help improve time management skills.
4. Personal reminders: Encourage your teen to set reminders on their phone or use a planner to keep track of assignments and deadlines.

Here's a simple self-monitoring checklist your teen can use:

Daily Focus Checklist:

- I prepared my study space before starting work
- I put my phone away during study time
- I took short breaks every 30 minutes
- I completed my most important task first
- I asked for help when I needed it

Encourage your teen to reflect on their checklist at the end of each day. What went well? What could be improved tomorrow?

Cognitive Behavioral Strategies

Cognitive Behavioral Therapy (CBT) techniques can be very helpful for teens with ADHD. While it's best to work with a trained therapist for full CBT, there are some strategies you can implement at home:

1. Thought stopping: Help your teen identify negative thought patterns and replace them with more positive, productive thoughts. For example, instead of "I can't do this, it's too hard," encourage them to think, "This is challenging, but I can break it down into smaller steps."
2. Cognitive restructuring: Teach your teen to challenge irrational thoughts and look for evidence that contradicts negative beliefs.
3. Mindfulness practices: Simple mindfulness exercises can help improve focus and reduce anxiety. Try guided meditations or deep breathing exercises with your teen.

The goal of these strategies is to help your teen develop better self-awareness and control over their thoughts and behaviors. It takes time and practice, so be patient and celebrate small improvements along the way.

Environmental Modifications

Sometimes, small changes to the environment can make a big difference in focus and productivity. Here are some modifications to consider:

1. Create a quiet study area: Designate a specific space for homework and studying, free from distractions like TV or high-traffic areas of the house.
2. Use visual aids: Implement visual schedules, to-do lists, or color-coded systems to help your teen stay organized.
3. Provide fidget tools: For teens who need to move to focus, provide stress balls, fidget spinners, or other quiet manipulatives.
4. Optimize lighting: Ensure the study area has good lighting to reduce eye strain and maintain alertness.
5. Consider noise-canceling headphones: These can be helpful for teens who are easily distracted by background noise.

Here's a quick activity to get your teen involved in optimizing their study space:

Study Space Makeover:

1. Have your teen list what distracts them most when studying.
2. Brainstorm solutions for each distraction.
3. Implement changes to the study space based on these solutions.
4. After a week, evaluate what's working and what needs further adjustment.

By involving your teen in this process, you're teaching them to be proactive about creating an environment that supports their focus and productivity.

What works for one teen might not work for another. The key is to experiment with different techniques and modifications until you find what works best for your teen. In the next section, we'll explore how school counselors can provide additional support and insights for teens with ADHD and executive functioning challenges.

Professional Insights from School Counselors

School counselors can be invaluable allies in supporting teens with ADHD and executive functioning challenges. They offer a unique perspective, seeing your teen in the school environment and understanding the academic and social demands they face. Let's explore how school counselors can help and what insights they can provide.

The Role of School Counselors

School counselors wear many hats when it comes to supporting teens with ADHD:

1. Academic support: They help students develop effective study habits, manage their time, and set achievable goals.
2. Emotional and social guidance: Counselors provide a safe space for teens to express their feelings and work through challenges.
3. Liaison between teachers and parents: They facilitate communication to ensure everyone is on the same page regarding your teen's needs and progress.
4. Advocate for accommodations: Counselors can help implement and adjust IEPs or 504 plans.

Counselor Strategies

School counselors have a toolkit of strategies to support executive functioning. Here are some common approaches:

1. Goal-setting sessions: Counselors help teens break down long-term goals into manageable steps. For example, if your teen wants to improve their grades, a counselor might help them set specific goals for each subject and create action plans to achieve them.
2. Time management workshops: These sessions teach students how to prioritize tasks, use planners effectively, and avoid procrastination.
3. Social skills groups: For teens who struggle with social aspects of ADHD (like impulsivity in conversations), these groups provide a safe space to practice social skills.

Here's an example of how a counselor might break down a goal with your teen:

Goal: Improve Math Grade from C to B

1. Attend all classes and pay attention (2 weeks)
2. Complete all homework assignments on time (1 month)
3. Seek help during teacher's office hours for difficult topics (ongoing)
4. Study for tests at least 3 days in advance (for each test)
5. Review progress with counselor bi-weekly

Collaborative Approach

The most effective support comes when school counselors, teachers, and parents work together. Here's how to foster this collaboration:

1. Regular communication: Set up a system for sharing updates, whether it's weekly emails or monthly check-ins.
2. Joint meetings: Attend meetings with your teen's counselor and teachers to discuss progress and challenges.
3. Shared responsibility: Work with the school team to determine who will handle different aspects of support. For example, the counselor might work on organizational strategies, while you focus on creating a structured home environment.

Accessing School Resources

School counselors can help you navigate the resources available at your teen's school. Here's what to ask about:

1. Assessments and evaluations: Schools can often provide or recommend evaluations to better understand your teen's needs.
2. Support groups: Many schools offer groups for students with ADHD or executive functioning challenges.
3. School-based interventions: Ask about programs like study skills classes or peer tutoring.
4. Community resources: Counselors often have information about local therapists, ADHD coaches, or support groups.

Here's a quick checklist for your next meeting with the school counselor:

School Counselor Meeting Checklist:

- Discuss current academic performance
- Review existing accommodations and their effectiveness
- Explore additional support options
- Set goals for the next term
- Schedule next check-in

School counselors are there to help. Don't hesitate to reach out and utilize their expertise in supporting your teen's executive functioning skills.

Leveraging Technology for Executive Functioning

In our digital age, technology can be both a blessing and a curse for teens with executive functioning challenges. When used mindfully, however, tech tools can significantly support organization, time management, and focus. Let's explore how to leverage technology effectively.

Educational Apps

There's an app for almost everything these days, including executive functioning support. Here are some top picks:

1. Todoist: A powerful task management app that helps break down projects, set deadlines, and track progress.
2. MyHomework Student Planner: Keeps track of classes, assignments, and tests with helpful reminders.
3. Evernote: Great for note-taking and organizing information across devices.

4. Forest: Encourages focus by gamifying the process of staying off your phone.

Encourage your teen to try different apps and find what works best for them. The key is consistency in using the chosen tools.

Assistive Technology

For teens who struggle with specific aspects of executive functioning, assistive technology can be game-changing:

1. Speech-to-text software: Helps teens who have difficulty with writing or typing to get their thoughts down quickly.
2. Text-to-speech tools: Can help with reading comprehension by allowing teens to listen to text.
3. Digital highlighters and annotation tools: Make it easier to organize and remember important information from digital texts.
4. Smart pens: Record audio while taking notes, allowing students to review lessons later.

Online Resources and Communities

The internet offers a wealth of resources for teens with ADHD and their parents:

1. ADDitude Magazine (additudemag.com): Offers articles, webinars, and forums on ADHD and executive functioning.
2. Understood.org: Provides information and strategies for learning and attention issues.
3. CHADD (chadd.org): Children and Adults with Attention-Deficit/Hyperactivity Disorder offers support and resources.

These online communities can provide valuable insights, support, and a sense of connection for both you and your teen.

Balancing Technology Use

While technology can be helpful, it's crucial to use it mindfully. Here are some tips for healthy tech habits:

1. Set screen time limits: Use built-in tools on devices or apps like OurPact to manage screen time.
2. Create tech-free zones: Designate certain areas (like the dinner table) or times as device-free.
3. Model good habits: Demonstrate healthy technology use yourself.
4. Encourage offline activities: Balance tech use with physical activities, face-to-face social time, and offline hobbies.

Here's a simple tech use agreement you can create with your teen:

Technology Use Agreement:

1. Homework time: Phones in a designated basket, only educational apps allowed on computer
2. Dinner time: No devices at the table
3. Bedtime: All devices charged outside the bedroom
4. Weekend reward: Extra 30 minutes of recreational screen time for meeting weekly goals

The goal is to use technology as a tool to enhance executive functioning, not as a crutch or distraction. With the right approach, tech can be a powerful ally in supporting your teen's development.

Creating a Supportive Home Environment

While school strategies and technology are important, the home environment plays a crucial role in supporting your teen's executive functioning skills. Let's explore how to create a home atmosphere that nurtures these skills.

Structuring the Home Environment

1. Establish consistent routines: Create a daily schedule that includes regular times for waking up, meals, homework, and bedtime. Consistency helps reduce anxiety and improves time management.
2. Create dedicated study spaces: Designate a quiet, well-lit area for homework and studying. Ensure it's stocked with necessary supplies and free from distractions.
3. Implement organizational systems: Use labeled bins, color-coded folders, or digital organization tools to keep everything in its place.
4. Visual reminders: Use whiteboards, bulletin boards, or digital displays to keep important information visible.

Here's a sample daily routine to consider:

6:30 AM - Wake up, morning routine 7:30 AM - Breakfast 8:00 AM - School 3:30 PM - After-school snack & short break 4:00 PM - Homework time 6:00 PM - Free time/extracurriculars 7:00 PM - Dinner 8:00 PM - Evening routine, pack bag for tomorrow 9:00 PM - Wind-down time (no screens) 9:30 PM - Bedtime

Family Involvement

1. Regular family meetings: Hold weekly meetings to discuss schedules, challenges, and successes.
2. Collaborative planning: Work with your teen to plan their week, set goals, and prioritize tasks.
3. Shared responsibilities: Assign household tasks to build a sense of responsibility and accomplishment.
4. Lead by example: Model good organizational and time management habits yourself.

Promoting Positive Behavior

1. Use praise effectively: Offer specific, sincere praise for effort and progress, not just outcomes.
2. Set clear expectations: Clearly communicate your expectations for behavior and responsibilities.
3. Consistent consequences: Follow through with agreed-upon consequences when expectations aren't met.
4. Reward system: Consider implementing a reward system for meeting goals or consistently following routines.

Providing Emotional Support

1. Practice active listening: Give your teen your full attention when they're speaking to you.
2. Validate feelings: Acknowledge your teen's emotions without judgment.
3. Encourage open communication: Create an environment where your teen feels safe sharing their thoughts and feelings.
4. Offer help, don't impose: Ask, "How can I support you?" instead of jumping in with solutions.

Remember, creating a supportive home environment is an ongoing process. Be patient with yourself and your teen as you work together to find what works best for your family.

Real-Life Case Study: Specialized Success Stories

Let's meet Jason, a 15-year-old diagnosed with ADHD. Jason struggled with staying focused on schoolwork, often felt overwhelmed by assignments, and had difficulty managing his time. His grades were slipping, and his confidence was waning.

Initial Challenges:

- Difficulty starting and completing homework
- Easily distracted in class
- Trouble organizing school materials
- Low self-esteem due to academic struggles

Strategies Implemented:

1. Personalized Learning Plan:
   - Extended time on tests
   - Use of a quiet study room for exams
   - Permission to use fidget tools in class
2. Behavioral Interventions:
   - Implemented a token economy system at home
   - Broke down assignments into smaller, manageable tasks
   - Used a timer for focused work sessions (Pomodoro Technique)
3. Technology Support:
   - Introduced a digital planner app for organizing assignments
   - Used text-to-speech software for reading assignments
   - Implemented website blockers during study time
4. Home Environment Changes:
   - Created a dedicated, clutter-free study space
   - Established a consistent daily routine
   - Implemented a visual schedule for daily tasks
5. School Collaboration:
   - Regular check-ins with school counselor
   - Teacher updates on assignment progress
   - Participation in a school-based social skills group

Challenges Faced:

- Initial resistance to new routines and tools
- Inconsistent use of strategies when stressed
- Difficulty balancing increased structure with desire for independence

Adjustments Made:

- Simplified digital planner to focus on most critical tasks
- Introduced short, frequent breaks during study sessions
- Gradually increased responsibility for managing own schedule

Positive Outcomes:

- Improved grades across all subjects
- Enhanced ability to start and complete assignments independently
- Increased confidence and positive self-image
- Better time management skills
- Improved relationships with teachers and peers

Key Takeaways from Jason's Story:

1. Personalized approach: What works for one teen may not work for another. Tailoring strategies to Jason's specific needs was crucial.
2. Consistency is key: Regular use of strategies, even when challenging, led to significant improvements over time.
3. Collaboration matters: Working together with school staff ensured consistent support across all environments.
4. Technology can be a powerful tool: When used mindfully, tech tools significantly supported Jason's organization and focus.

5. Patience and flexibility are essential: Progress wasn't linear, and strategies needed adjustment along the way.
6. Building on successes: Small wins boosted Jason's confidence, motivating him to continue using helpful strategies.

Jason's journey demonstrates that with the right support and strategies, teens with ADHD can overcome executive functioning challenges and thrive both academically and personally.

Wrapping Up

As we conclude this chapter, remember that supporting a teen with executive functioning challenges is a journey, not a destination. It requires patience, consistency, and a willingness to adapt. Here are some final thoughts to keep in mind:

1. Celebrate progress: Acknowledge and appreciate improvements, no matter how small.
2. Stay flexible: Be ready to adjust strategies as your teen's needs evolve.
3. Maintain open communication: Keep the dialogue open with your teen, their teachers, and other support professionals.
4. Take care of yourself: Supporting a teen with executive functioning challenges can be demanding. Make sure to practice self-care and seek support when needed.
5. Keep learning: Stay informed about new strategies and resources that could benefit your teen.

By implementing the strategies we've discussed - from personalized learning plans to leveraging technology and creating a supportive home environment - you're providing your teen with the tools they need to succeed. Remember, the goal isn't perfection, but progress and increased independence.

A Chance to Pay It Forward

As you turn the last pages of this book, please take a moment to hold the door open for someone else – for another parent that may be experiencing similar challenges with their teen.

Simply by sharing one to two sentences about your own journey with your teen, you'll show new readers where they can find all the guidance they need to boost their teens' executive functioning skills too.

Please scan the QR code to leave a review.

Thank you so much for your support. We're all on our own parenting journey, but every ounce of help we can share makes a huge impact to our future generation.

Conclusion

As we reach the end of our journey through the world of executive functioning skills, let's take a moment to reflect on why these skills are so crucial for your teen's success, both now and in the future.

Think of executive functioning skills as the control center of your teen's brain. They're the skills that help your teen:

- Plan and organize their day
- Focus on important tasks
- Remember key information
- Juggle multiple responsibilities
- Make good decisions
- Regulate their emotions

By helping your teen develop these skills, you're not just setting them up for academic success - you're equipping them with tools they'll use throughout their lives.

Throughout this book, we've broken down complex concepts into manageable pieces. Let's recap some of the key takeaways:

1. Understanding Executive Functioning: We've explored what these skills are and why they matter.
2. Getting Organized: We've discussed tools like daily planners, checklists, and the power of a clutter-free environment.
3. Time Management: Remember the Pomodoro Technique? We've covered strategies to help your teen make the most of their time.
4. Emotional Regulation: We've explored techniques for managing stress and building resilience.
5. Enhancing Focus: From creating distraction-free zones to understanding the importance of sleep and nutrition, we've covered ways to boost attention.
6. Goal Setting and Prioritization: We've talked about setting SMART goals and balancing short-term and long-term objectives.
7. Parent-Teen Collaboration: We've discussed how to communicate effectively and work together with your teen.
8. Specialized Strategies: For teens with ADHD or other challenges, we've explored tailored approaches and professional insights.

Remember, improving executive functioning skills is a journey, not a destination. It's okay if your teen doesn't master everything at once. The key is consistent effort and patience.

Here's a simple plan to get started:

1. Choose one strategy from the book to implement this week.
2. Discuss it with your teen and agree on how you'll put it into practice.
3. Try it out for a week, then reflect together on what worked and what didn't.
4. Adjust as needed and keep going!
5. After a month, choose another strategy to add to your toolkit.

Remember to celebrate small victories along the way. Did your teen remember to use their planner all week? That's worth a high five! Did they break down a big project into smaller steps? Time for a special treat!

As we wrap up, I want to thank you for your commitment to your teen's growth. Your dedication is the foundation of their success. With the right strategies and consistent support, every teen has the potential to develop strong executive functioning skills.

Remember, you're not just helping your teen succeed in school - you're setting them up for a lifetime of success. Whether they're managing a complex project at work, juggling family responsibilities, or pursuing their dreams, the skills you're helping them develop now will serve them well into the future.

Thank you for allowing me to be a part of this journey with you. Here's to your teen's bright and promising future!

References

ActiveCollab. (n.d.). 8 steps to break down tasks into manageable pieces. https://activecollab.com/blog/project-management/break-down-tasks

Asana. (n.d.). The Eisenhower Matrix: How to prioritize your to-do list. https://asana.com/resources/eisenhower-matrix

Bright Futures NY. (n.d.). How to help teens manage academic pressure. https://www.brightfuturesny.com/post/help-teens-manage-academic-pressure

Business.com. (n.d.). Best tools for setting and tracking goals. https://www.business.com/articles/11-best-tools-for-setting-and-tracking-goals/

Center on the Developing Child at Harvard University. (n.d.). What is executive function? How does it relate to child development? https://developingchild.harvard.edu/resources/what-is-executive-function-and-how-does-it-relate-to-child-development/

Child Mind Institute. (n.d.). Tips for communicating with your teen. https://childmind.org/article/tips-communicating-with-teen/

College of Western Idaho. (n.d.). What is the Pomodoro Technique? A college student's guide. https://cwi.edu/news/blog/what-pomodoro-technique-college-students-guide

Cortés Pascual, A., Moyano Muñoz, N., & Quílez Robres, A. (2019). The Relationship Between Executive Functions and Academic Performance in Primary Education: Review and Meta-Analysis. *Frontiers in Psychology, 10*(10). https://doi.org/10.3389/fpsyg.2019.01582

DuPaul, G. J., Kern, L., Belk, G., Custer, B., Daffner, M., Hatfield, A., & Peek, D. (2018). Face-to-face versus online behavioral parent training for young children at risk for ADHD: Treatment engagement and outcomes. Journal of Clinical Child & Adolescent Psychology, 47(sup1), S369-S383. https://doi.org/10.1080/15374416.2017.1342544

Edutopia. (n.d.). Teaching more efficiently with checklists. https://www.edutopia.org/article/using-checklists-classroom-enhance-efficiency/

Family Education. (n.d.). 22 super helpful apps for kids with ADHD. https://www.familyeducation.com/kids/neurodiversity/adhd/22-super-helpful-apps-for-kids-with-adhd

Gottman Institute. (n.d.). Building trust with teenagers. https://www.gottman.com/blog/building-trust-with-teenagers/

Independent. (n.d.). 7 expert tips to help kids and teens declutter. https://www.independent.co.uk/life-style/teenagers-joy-b2196710.html

Life Skills Advocate. (n.d.). 13 practical time management skills to teach teens. https://lifeskillsadvocate.com/blog/13-practical-time-management-skills-to-teach-teens/

Lilac Center. (n.d.). 8 tips on how to help a teen regulate their emotions. https://www.lilaccenter.org/blog/8-tips-on-how-to-help-a-teen-regulate-their-emotions

Madore, K. P., & Wagner, A. D. (2019). Multicosts of Multitasking. *Cerebrum: The Dana Forum on Brain Science, 2019.* https://www.ncbi.nlm.nih.gov/pmc/articles/PMC7075496/

Mindset Works. (n.d.). How parents can instill a growth mindset at home. https://www.mindsetworks.com/parents/growth-mindset-parenting

Pathway College. (n.d.). How to create a distraction-free study zone. https://www.pathwayscollege.edu/online-college-pasadena/how-to-create-a-distraction-free-study-zone-2/

Psychology Today. (2022, October 3). 8 ways to help your teen stop procrastinating. https://www.psychologytoday.com/us/blog/promoting-empathy-your-teen/202210/8-ways-help-your-teen-stop-procrastinating

Raising Children Network. (n.d.). Conflict management with pre-teens and teenagers. https://raisingchildren.net.au/teens/communicating-relationships/communicating/conflict-management-with-teens

River Software. (n.d.). Balancing act: How to manage short term and long term goals. https://www.riversoftware.com/productivity/balancing-act-how-to-manage-short-term-and-long-term-goals/

Sabrina's Organizing. (n.d.). Teen academic planner to master time management. https://sabrinasorganizing.com/academic-planner-for-teens/

Smart Kids with Learning Disabilities. (n.d.). Teens and executive function skills. https://www.smartkidswithld.org/getting-help/executive-function-disorder/teens-and-executive-function-skills/

Teaching Channel. (n.d.). Bite-sized goal setting with micro-goals. https://www.teachingchannel.com/k12-hub/downloadable/bite-sized-goal-setting-with-micro-goals/

The Blue Heart Foundation. (n.d.). SMART goals and your teen. https://theblueheartfoundation.org/smart-goals-and-your-teen/

U.S. Department of Health & Human Services. (n.d.). Joint planning. https://eclkc.ohs.acf.hhs.gov/family-engagement/home-visitors-online-handbook/joint-planning

Understood. (n.d.). 10 common executive function assessments parents should know about. https://adayinourshoes.com/executive-function-assessment/